ENDANGERED SPECIES

# CROCODILES AND ALLIGATORS

ENDANGERED SPECIES

# CROCODILES AND ALLIGATORS

CHARLES LEVY

THE APPLE PRESS

A QUINTET BOOK

Published by The Apple Press
6 Blundell Street
London N7 9BH

ISBN 1-85076-328-3

This book was designed and produced by
Quintet Publishing Limited
6 Blundell Street
London N7 9BH

Creative Director: Terry Jeavons
Designer: Peter Radcliffe
Project Editor: Sally Harper
Editor: Michele Staple
Artworker: Danny McBride

Typeset in Great Britain by
Central Southern Typesetters, Eastbourne
Manufactured in Hong Kong by
Regent Publishing Services Limited
Printed in Hong Kong by
Leefung-Ascc Printers Limited

# CONTENTS

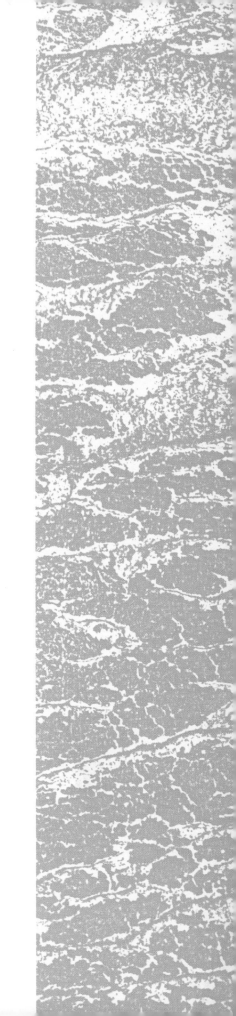

# FOREWORD

For 190 million years before the first humans evolved, huge populations of crocodilians, in more or less their present form, inhabited the waters and shorelines of rivers, lakes, swamps and estuaries of tropical and subtropical lands. Today they represent the last true survivors of the huge reptiles that once dominated the seas and land masses of Earth for over 200 million years. Not only did they survive the great extinctions that saw the demise of the dinosaurs and many other species of plants and animals, but because of their size, strength and armour, as adults they were relatively invulnerable.

With the appearance of *Homo sapiens sapiens*, the destinies of the crocodilians and humans inextricably meshed. Humans required water for drinking, cooking, bathing, transport and, once they had domesticated wild animals, livestock. In early times, humans in competition with crocodiles for water resources usually came out the losers. From the dawn of recorded history, crocodiles and alligators were incorporated into creation myths and fables, and even became objects of deification, reaching a pinnacle with the Egyptian crocodile god, Sobek. They were also viewed with fear, loathing and hatred. Early hunting efforts, however, made no significant impression on the endemic populations of crocodiles and alligators, until primitive lands were colonized and hunters with high-powered, accurately sighted rifles appeared on the scene.

Hunting for sport had little impact until it became commercially profitable to kill crocodilians for their skins. The 'skins game' and other commercial enterprises, such as selling young crocodiles, alligators and caymans for pets, or killing and stuffing them to be sold as novelty items, brought the world crocodilian populations to the verge of extinction. In the short span of 60 years these magnificent animals that had survived for millions of years were almost wiped out.

Humans pride themselves on their wisdom, and a worldwide effort to save endangered wildlife attests to that attribute. Hopefully, these measures will not be too little or too late. In zoos, national parks, government-sponsored reserves, and private ranches and farms, endangered species of crocodilians are being bred and studied by a small but dedicated group of biologists. Governments too have enacted legislation and joined in an international effort to regulate the skin trade, preserve natural habitats and reintroduce species to their original domains. It is to the dedicated crocodilian biologists such as Romulus Whittaker of the Madras Crocodile Bank in India, John Behler of the New York Bronx Zoo Captive Breeding Program, Jeff Lang of the University of North Dakota, Charles Ross of the Smithsonian Institution and Kent Vliet of the University of Florida that I dedicate this book.

# THE
# LIVING
# DINOSAURS

Most people in the Western world have never seen a live crocodilian, save for the motionless, apparently lethargic specimens kept in zoos. Yet all of us, from an early age, have a rough idea of what a crocodile or alligator is, thanks to their frequent appearances in children's fables, books and cartoons. We all remember the 'croc who swallowed the clock' in J.M. Barrie's *Peter Pan* and its relentless *tic-tic-tic* as it doggedly pursued the hero's arch enemy Captain Hook. Disney Studios produced both films and comic books featuring crocodiles, among which were Donald Duck's adventures as a crocodile collector. Rudyard Kipling made many references to crocodiles in his *Just So Stories* for children, but none had more impact than his fable of how the elephant got its trunk in *The Elephant's Child*. In most of these stories the crocodile is portrayed as a large, toothy and malevolent creature, but some children's stories treat them as benign and lovable. Of course, neither representation is true.

Part of our fascination for crocodiles is the opportunity they give us for seeing the only living representatives of the huge dinosaurs that ruled the planet for some 140 million years. But what exactly is a crocodilian? How do they function? Are they really man-eaters? How do they affect us (and vice versa)? The aim of this book is to provide a complete picture of modern crocodilians and a greater appreciation of their unique place in history. Unfortunately, in the short span of less than a hundred

*RIGHT:* When seen in captivity, even a large crocodilian such as this American alligator can seem a docile and unaggressive creature.

years, humans have almost obliterated these extraordinary beasts. Despite surviving the great extinctions of the dinosaurs, the ice ages that eliminated many of the large mammals, such as the woolly mammoth, the mastedon, the giant cave bear and the sabre-tooth cat, and outlasting all of our early ancestors (*Australopithecus*, *Homo erectus*, *Homo sapiens neanderthalis*), the future of the crocodilians now seems in doubt.

Of the 22 species alive today, 17 are on the verge of extinction. Fortunately, humans have at last recognized what a great evolutionary loss this would be and have embarked on some promising attempts to preserve all 22 species for future generations. These efforts are discussed in Chapter 7.

## THE PLACE OF CROCODILIANS IN THE ORDER OF LIFE

It is because humans have orderly and inquisitive minds that we have devised a filing system for all living things, to enforce some form of order on the chaos created by the existence of several million different species of organisms. This system follows an evolutionary time-scale and groups organisms by similarities in structure, embryonic development, metabolism and biochemistry, as well as in the molecular biology of their hereditary material, DNA. Currently, organisms are grouped into five distinct kingdoms: the monera (blue-green algae and bacteria); the protists (unicellular organisms of a more complex cell structure); the fungi; the plants; and

the animals. Within each kingdom there are further subdivisions based on a hier-archical order, most ancient to most recent. Thus, crocodilians belong to the animal kingdom in the phylum Chordata – animals that at some time in their life, embryonic or adult, had gill slits and a dorsal rod of embryonic mesoderm, a notochord. From the chordates arose the subphylum Verte-brata, or animals with backbones. Among the various vertebrates the crocodilians fall within the class Rep-tilia, which comprises those organisms sharing common reptilian character-istics. Within a given class there are orders and crocodilians belong to the order Crocodylia, those animals sharing common crocodilian traits. Many of this order are extinct, and are known only from the fossil record. Thus, we can look back in time about 200 million years and find ancestors of the modern crocodilians of the suborder Eusuchia. The Eusuchia can further be subdivided into the family Crocodylidae to which all modern crocodilians belong, fitting into one of three subfamilies: the Crocodylinae (crocodiles), consisting of 14 species, 10 of which are considered endangered; the subfamily Alligator-inae, consisting of seven species, two of which are endangered; and the sub-family Gavialinae, which consists of only one species (and that one is considered endangered).

## EVOLUTION OF MODERN CROCODILIANS

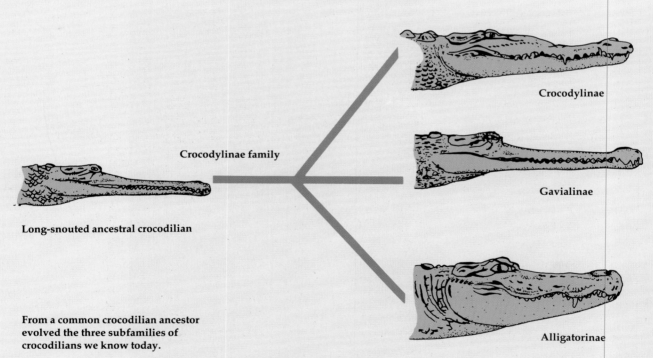

**Crocodylinae family**

**Long-snouted ancestral crocodilian**

**Crocodylinae**

**Gavialinae**

**Alligatorinae**

**From a common crocodilian ancestor evolved the three subfamilies of crocodilians we know today.**

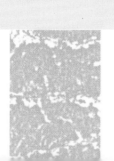

BELOW: This American alligator's head-on dental display gives some appreciation of the power of its bite. The teeth are conical and vary in size. Old teeth are shed and replaced by new teeth; in a lifetime an alligator will grow 2–3,000 teeth.

## WHAT'S IN A NAME?

Technical names in biology are in large part based on Latin and Greek roots, prefixes and suffixes. The word crocodile has its origin with the early Greek visitors to Egypt who thought the large Nile crocodiles looked like a small Greek lizard *krokodilos* (*kroke* = pebble; *drilos* = worm); hence, the common name crocodile. The scientific name for the suborder of modern crocodilians comes from the suffix *suchia*, derived from the Greek root *souchos*, itself a corruption of the Egyptians' name for their crocodile god Sobek, Sebek or Sbek, and *eu* meaning 'true'. Thus true crocodiles: Eusuchia. The long-snouted gharyal's name is derived from the Hindi or Nepali word *ghariyal*, in its turn derived from or akin to the Sanskrit *ghantika* (alligator). The fact that *gharyal* was in use long before *haryial* did not affect the rules of scientific name-calling for many years. The name *gharyal* has been restored even though taxonomy decrees that the first name that appears in the published literature should persist. Similarly, errors in spelling are also retained; hence *Alligator mississipiensis* was the name used until recently, although 'Mississippi' is actually spelt with two 'p's.

## THE EXTERNAL ANATOMY OF A CROCODILIAN

All 22 species of modern crocodilians are cold-blooded, amphibious, egg-laying reptiles covered with discontinuous horny scales. Their elongated bodies are supported by four legs, the front pair of which is shorter than the hind pair. All four feet have five digits (toes) and are slightly webbed to provide a larger surface area for traction when

*ABOVE:* Threat is a much more economical way of defending a territory than actual fighting because it requires less energy and poses no risk to the defender. Here, a large American alligator sends a very unambiguous threat signal.

*FACING PAGE, ABOVE:* Alligators have very broad snouts and when their mouths are closed the pair of large teeth (fourth from the front of the lower jaw) fit into a cavity inside the upper jaw.

*FACING PAGE, BELOW:* The long fourth tooth on the crocodile's upper jaw sits outside the jaw when the mouth is closed, as this shot of a Nile crocodile shows.

walking on land. Upon close inspection the hindlegs seem to have only four digits, with the three innermost bearing strong claws. This is because the fifth toe is miniature and only partially developed, being a remnant of the evolutionary past. All crocodilians bear flattened, long, tooth-lined skulls of variable shape and size (according to the species' primary food source). The longest, narrowest snouts with the most teeth are found in the fish-eating gharyals (*Gavialis gangeticus*). Their mouths are lined with about a hundred, even-sized, conical teeth. The false gharyal, *Tomistoma schlegelii*, a distant relative of the gharyal, has a similar appearance, but some anatomists are of

the opinion that it belongs to the crocodile subfamily, Crocodylinae. There are also several species of narrow-snouted crocodiles whose tooth sizes vary. Other crocodiles have broader snouts, but they can be distinguished from alligators (which tend to have the broadest snouts) by the long fourth tooth of the lower jaw that sits in a groove on the outside of the upper jaw when the mouth is closed. In alligators, this tooth is not visible when the jaws are shut, as it is accommodated in a bony pit on the upper jaw. This is the simplest way to differentiate between crocodiles and alligators. All crocodilians have long, muscular tails that they use to propel themselves through the water.

## MUSCULOSKELETAL SYSTEM

The elongated crocodilian skull is composed of a number of fused bones. Both the upper and lower jaws have numerous open-rooted teeth set in deep sockets. Each pointed tooth is conical and is held firmly in its socket with connective tissue. In gharyals the teeth are all approximately the same size, but in alligators and crocodiles the teeth show some size differentiation, particularly the larger fourth pair of teeth in the lower jaw.

Each tooth is replaced about every two years, with the teeth in front being replaced more frequently than those in the rear. Replacement of teeth in young crocodiles starts at the back of the jaws, but in older crocodiles replacement starts at the front. Episodes of tooth replacement occur in waves, with newly differentiating teeth migrating up into the hollow base of the old tooth. The remnants of the root of the old tooth are reabsorbed while the thick-walled crowns are shed. Throughout its lifetime a large crocodile may grow several thousand teeth.

The upper jaw and lower jaw articulate (are jointed) at the very rear of the skull, allowing the animals to open their jaws very wide. Behind the bones that make up the orbit of the eye the rear portion of the cheek bones are perforated by two openings that are thought to play a role in permitting the powerful muscles that close the jaw to bulge during contraction. These ridged apertures also serve as bony attachments for these muscles. The muscles that close the jaw are so strong that during a snap the pressure generated can be several thousand pounds per square inch. The muscles that open the jaw are considerably weaker, and a strong man can hold a large crocodile's mouth shut with his bare hands. Only the lower jaw moves downward, although when observing a basking crocodile with its mouth agape it appears that the upper jaw has lifted.

Crocodilian necks are relatively short, being made up of nine cervical vertebrae, some of which have floating ribs. The chest cage is made up of 10 rib-bearing thoracic vertebrae, the tenth being a floating rib and the other nine jointed to a plate-like breastbone or sternum. The muscles between the ribs allow the chest cage to expand, thereby decreasing the pressure in the chest cavity and abetting the flow of air into the lungs. Crocodilians were the first animals to have a sheet-like muscular diaphragm separating the chest cavity from the abdominal cavity. Movements of the diaphragm also play a role in causing inspiration and expiration of air from the lungs.

Continuing along the spine, crocodilians have five lumbar, two sacral and

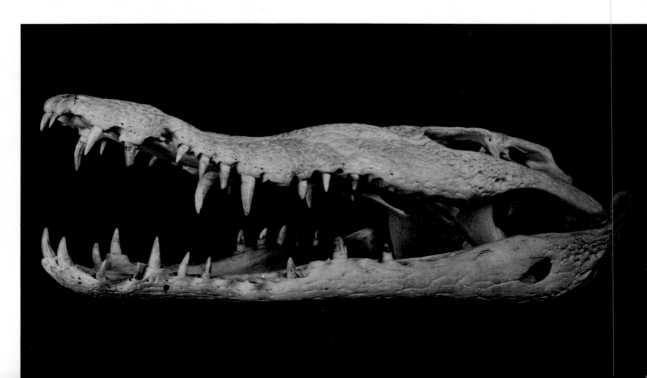

ABOVE: An American
crocodile in the high
walk mode of
locomotion. The
partially webbed feet
provide a broad
surface area, which
is useful for walking
over muddy
surfaces.

35 caudal (tail) vertebrae. Embedded in the sides of the ventral body wall are dermal ribs which do not attach to the skeleton. Anteriorly, the pectoral girdle, into which the short, stout forelimbs articulate, attaches to the sternum. The longer rear limbs articulate with the pelvic girdle and terminate in four visible digits, all of which tend to be much longer than those of the forelimb.

## LOCOMOTION

The muscles of the limbs are sufficiently strong to allow the animal to stand with its belly off the ground, to walk and, in some species, to run at a gallop for short distances on land. In the water the limbs are usually held back against the body, giving the swimming crocodilian a streamlined torpedo shape, but they may also be used as rudders to effect a change in direction. The largest muscle mass is found on the long, somewhat laterally flattened tail, the undulations of which provide the main propulsive force during swimming.

On land the larger crocodilians have two basic modes of movement: an unhurried, stately walk, with belly and much of the tail completely off the ground and legs held almost vertically beneath the body; and a rather undignified belly-crawl, which they use to lurch

LEFT: The muscles
that close the jaws of
a large American
alligator can
generate a pressure
of several thousand
pounds per square
inch but the muscles
that open the jaw are
relatively weak.
Here one researcher
holds the jaws shut
while his co-workers
prepare to do a
sperm count.

*ABOVE:* A common cayman walks along a sand bar in the Peruvian Amazon. In the high walk the animal's trunk and most of its tail is held off the ground. In this mode of locomotion maximum speed is about 5 kph (3 mph); surprisingly, though, these animals may walk great distances overland.

forward at speed. The former high walk allows them to traverse considerable distances, albeit rather slowly. Walking quickly and purposefully, a large alligator or crocodile can reach a maximal speed of about 5 kph (3 mph). This gait, like that of four-footed mammals, alternately moves the left forelimb and right hindlimb together, followed by movement of the right forelimb and left hindlimb, thereby providing a stable platform. When in a hurry the shift is made to a trot in which both fore- and hindlimbs move almost simultaneously. However, the larger species are rather poorly co-ordinated at this faster pace and usually sprawl awkwardly on to their bellies with limbs splayed to the sides. Forward motion continues as the body thrashes from side to side, the limbs acting like oars. This so-called belly-crawl is often seen when startled

crocodiles plunge from their basking sites on the shore into the water. The belly-crawl is also used when the crocodile stealthily slips into the water in pursuit of prey.

Some smaller crocodiles can actually effect a high-speed gallop that uses the more powerful hindlimbs to thrust the body forward with forelimbs extended. This sort of bounding gait can, for short distances, carry the crocodile forward at about 16 kph (10 mph), still hardly a high speed for humans. For example, world-class male sprinters have been clocked at 43 kph (27 mph).

## CARDIOVASCULAR AND PULMONARY SYSTEMS

The evolution of a highly efficient four-chambered heart, such as that found in modern mammals and birds, first occurred in crocodilians. The heart is divided into two (right and left) separate muscular pumping systems, the main difference between mammals and crocodilians in this regard being the presence of a connection or valve-like window, the foramen of Panizzae, between the right and left aortae. When the crocodile is at rest, resistance to blood flow to the lungs is low, consequently the right ventricle generates less pressure in the left ventricle. When this condition exists the blood pressure in the left systemic aorta is higher than that generated by the right ventricle, and the valve between the atrium, right ventricle and right aorta and the left aorta remains closed, thereby causing the oxygen-poor blood ejected from the contracting right ventricle to flow to the lungs for oxygen-ation. In this situation the crocodilian heart functions just like a human heart.

However, when the reptile dives, breathing stops. Then the resistance to flow in the pulmonary circuit increases to the point that the pressure in the right ventricle increases, exceeding the pressure in the left systemic aorta. When this happens the valve of the foramen of Panizzae opens and blood is shunted from the right heart into the left systemic aorta.

Crocodiles, like humans, have an adjustable supply-and-demand system for shunting blood to metabolically active tissues or for shunting blood to or from the peripheral circulation where heat exchange can occur. The shunting and pumping of blood is regulated by neural centres in the brain. The cardiac centres can change the rate and strength of contraction and thus increase or decrease the volume of blood being pumped, while the vasomotor centre regulates the diameter of the small arterioles, thereby controlling blood flow. If the animal gets too cold the peripheral circulation shuts down, thereby limiting heat loss. Conversely, if the animal overheats surface vessels reflexively dilate and blood is shunted to the surface to enhance cooling. During diving crocodilians can also adjust blood flow, ensuring that critical active organs such as the brain and heart get enough oxygenated blood while other organs get just enough oxygenated blood to maintain themselves.

The nostrils of all crocodilians are set in a slightly raised protuberance on the upper surface of the tips of their long snouts. The nostrils are equipped with muscular flaps which are under

neural control and can be closed when the animals submerge. These nostrils lead to a long, moist airway that extends the length of the skull and is separated from the mouth by a bony secondary palate at the rear of the skull. This passageway for air is also protected by a fleshy flap that, together with a flap at the rear of the tongue, acts like a valve to prevent water from entering the trachea, the airway to the lungs. Each crocodilian lung is enclosed within its own chamber within the thoracic cavity and, like the lung of a mammal, is highly compartmentalized, thereby providing a large surface area for the exchange of gases between the blood and the air in the lungs. Breathing is accomplished by movements of the ribs and diaphragm which, during inhalation (inspiration), produce a negative pressure causing air to flow passively into the lungs. During exhalation (expir-

*ABOVE:* Behavioural changes are the primary means of crocodilian temperature regulation. This Nile crocodile is basking in the sun on the banks of the upper Nile River in Uganda. Mouth gaping provides a major surface for heat exchange (see page 24).

ation), movements of the ribs and diaphragm increase the pressure around the lungs, pushing air out. As long as the snout is above the water's surface, a crocodilian can breathe perfectly efficiently even when the rest of its body is submerged.

## METABOLISM OF CROCODILIANS

All cold-blooded animals produce and use less energy than warm-blooded animals. The total energy input and output is referred to as the metabolic rate, and such rates can be measured with relative ease. The recent (1989) detailed studies of R.A. Coulson and his associates demonstrated that the metabolic rates of captive American alligators kept at a constant temperature varied with the volume of oxygen-rich blood being pumped per unit time per unit weight. Of course, in these cold-blooded creatures as body temperatures fall so does the metabolic rate. In a comparison of resting metabolic rates of a human and an alligator of the same weight, the alligator requires only 4% as many calories as the human. However, during maximal exertion or after feeding, the alligator can temporarily increase its metabolic rate by as much as 300%.

The low metabolic rate of adult crocodilians has another advantage in that it allows them to remain submerged for long periods of time, up to an hour, and still provide enough oxygen to their brains. As crocodilians increase in size, their brain growth does not keep pace, thus adult crocodilians have proportionally smaller brains compared with their young. Young crocodilians also have a

higher metabolic rate, and as a result can only stay submerged for a few minutes. The young grow much more rapidly than their elders too, and while crocodiles continue to grow throughout their lifetime, growth rate progressively declines. If one calculates the resting metabolism of one of these big, adult 500-kg (half-ton) alligators, one is startled to find that such an animal can maintain itself on a food intake of only 190 calories per day.

Crocodilians are extremely efficient in converting ingested food into energy supplies needed to maintain metabolism. The stomach, which has an extraordinarily acidic secretion, is capable of digesting even the protein in bones, and most of this protein, when metabolized, is stored in fat depots throughout the body. These fat stores provide a readily available reserve source of energy that can be mobilized on demand

*ABOVE:* A female gharyal showing the elongated snout which contains about 100 even-sized conical teeth. The thin snout is ideal for the rapid sideways movements used to catch fish, the gharial's primary food source.

when food is scarce. Young crocodilians have enough stored energy reserves to last a few months without feeding, while very large adults can last for well over a year. However, during bursts of activity (when hunting and feeding), metabolic rates are comparable to those of humans. This activity is mainly anaerobic and results in the accumulation of lactose in the blood (known as an oxygen debt). Elevated lactic acid levels in the blood mean that crocodilians tire easily; however, crocodilians can tolerate changes in blood acidity better than most animals.

How large animals grow is in part determined by their genetic make-up. Some species of crocodilians are relatively small while others are programmed for gargantuan proportions. Being cold-blooded, growth is also determined by environmental temperature and the availability of food. In young, rapidly metabolizing crocodilians, the growth rate in the first five or six years of life is very pronounced, and well-fed young can increase in size at the rate of about 30 cm (12 in) per year (less for the

*BELOW:* These brightly coloured American alligator hatchlings are basking on a branch over water covered with duckweed. At the approach of a predator they will splash into the water and hide under the duckweed.

smaller species). As they grow older their growth rate gradually declines, but nevertheless continues for as long as they live. This raises two questions: just how big can large crocodilians grow? and, how long do they live?

There are currently no age-specific data for any species of crocodilians living in the wild, but there are some documented age records for animals in captivity. From these limited reports it is possible to conclude that some of the larger reptiles can expect to live to a reasonable old age. One American alligator survived 56 years of captivity, and a Chinese alligator lived for 50 years. Captive crocodiles appear also to enjoy as great a longevity. A Nile crocodile in the Cairo Zoo lived for 40 years, and two Indian gharyals in the London Zoo survived for more than 30 years. The relationship of longevity of animals in captivity may not be really relevant to that of populations in the wild; however, given that they continue to grow for their entire term of life and that large adults suffer little predation, it is safe to say that some of the largest crocodiles are very old indeed. One expert estimates that some of the giant specimens described in the literature must be over 100 years old.

The relative average and maximal sizes of the 22 species of living crocodilians are summarized in the table on the right. Size, like any other biological variable, follows a normal, bell-shaped distribution curve. In a population of the same age and sex, 95% of the population will fall within two standard deviations of the mean or average size. At the extremes of the curve one would expect to find a few very small and a

| ADULT SIZES OF MODERN CROCODILIANS | | |
|---|---|---|
| **Common Name and Species** | **Average Size (in feet)*** | **Largest Ever Recorded**** |
| CUVIER'S DWARF CAYMAN (C. palpebrosus) | 4–5 | |
| SCHNEIDER'S DWARF CAYMAN (C. brigonatus) | 4.5–5.5 | |
| CHINESE ALLIGATOR (A. sinensis) | 4.5–6.5 | 10 |
| AFRICAN DWARF CROCODILE (O. tetraspis) | 5.5–6.5 | |
| COMMON CAYMAN (C. crocodilus) | 6–8 | 10 |
| BROAD-SNOUTED CAYMAN (C. latirostris) | 6.5–11.5 | |
| PHILIPPINE CROCODILE (C. mindorensis) | 7–9 | |
| JOHNSTON'S CROCODILE (C. johnsoni) | 7–10 | |
| CUBAN CROCODILE (C. rhombifer) | 8.5–11.5 | 16 |
| MORELET'S CROCODILE (C. moreletii) | 9.5–11.5 | |
| FALSE GHARIAL (T. schlegelii) | 9.8–13 | 13+ |
| SIAMESE CROCODILE (C. siamensis) | 10–13 | 13 |
| AFRICAN SLENDER-SNOUTED CROCODILE (C. cataphractes) | 10–13 | |
| NEW GUINEA CROCODILE (C. novaeguineae) | 10–13 | |
| MUGGER CROCODILE (C. palustris) | 10–13 | |
| AMERICAN ALLIGATOR (A. mississipiensis) | 10–16.5 | 20 |
| BLACK CAYMAN (M. niger) | 10–20 | |
| AMERICAN CROCODILE (C. acutus) | 11–20 | |
| NILE CROCODILE (C. niloticus) | 12–18 | 24 |
| ORINOCO CROCODILE (C. intermedius) | 18–20 | 23 |
| GHARIAL (G. gangeticus) | 18–21 | 30 |
| INDOPACIFIC CROCODILE (C. porosus) | 20–23 | 24+ |

\* Note that in most species, adult males are larger than adult females.
\*\* Data given where available; maximum sizes in historical records may be unreliable.

few very large individuals. The smaller ones are at some risk, but the larger ones, given their size, strength and armour are relatively invulnerable.

Humans are measurers. We are intrigued by size, and, in the recent history of human/crocodilian encounters since 1900, we have both anecdotal reports from hunters and measurements made and confirmed by scientists. In this book it is assumed that the hunters' measurements were indeed correct, although one should bear in mind the

*FACING PAGE, BELOW:* The genes for skin colour sometimes occur in pairs, resulting in albino organisms. In the wild this American alligator hatchling would probably be eaten since it would make a highly visible target for predators.

*FACING PAGE, ABOVE:* This mugger crocodile in Delhi Zoo can expect a long life, judging from other captive specimens which have lived for as long as 40 years.

human penchant for exaggeration. In the table shown here some of these measurements have been excluded, but it is instructive to record a few of them. The explorer Alexander von Humboldt reported sighting 7.3-m (24-ft) long Orinoco crocodiles, and Raymond Dittmar, Director of Reptiles of the New York Zoological Society, reported that he had shot an Indian gharyal 9 m (30 ft) long. In 1903 Mr H. Besser, hunting along the Mbaka River in what is now Tanzania, claimed to have shot and killed a Nile crocodile that was 7.6 m (25 ft) long, despite missing some of its tail, and whose skull measured 1.4 m (4.6 ft). While some of these extreme figures are questionable, there is no doubt about the existence of a giant but now extinct genus of crocodilian. Fossil remains of this giant have

been found in both the eastern and western United States, and recently an almost complete skull was discovered in Texas.

This giant thrived during the Cretaceous period, the Age of the Dinosaurs, and was actually called *Phobosuchus* (Gr. *phobos* fear + *souchos* crocodile). Recently, this now-extinct member of subfamily Crocodylinae was renamed *Deinosuchus* (Gr. *deinos* terrible). This terrordile probably reached a maximum length of 12 m (40 ft) and weighed several tons. One fossil skull measured 1.8 m (6 ft) in length. Fossil remains of this denizen of the Cretaceous waters are often found along with those of the duck-billed dinosaur, *Hadrosaurus*. This was a creature of some 9–12 m (30–40 ft), that was most probably preyed upon by *Deinosuchus*.

# DISTRIBUTION OF MODERN CROCODILIANS

The 22 species of living crocodilians are widely distributed throughout the tropical and semitropical parts of the world. How they got there is still a matter of controversy. Certainly, some of the theories of the dispersal of the eusuchian (true crocodilian) ancestral line can be explained in terms of continental drift. The evidence for the existence of a single large and continuous supercontinent called Pangea over 200 million years ago is overwhelming. At the end of the Triassic period, 200 million years ago, the ancestral true crocodilians had already appeared. Later, during the start of the Jurassic period, Pangea began to break apart and land masses that make up today's

*BELOW:* A reconstruction of a scene from the Cretaceous period: a Deinosuchus erupts from the water to attack two duckbilled Hadrosaurus dinosaurs. Deinosuchus was a giant crocodilian, reaching lengths of up to 12 m (40 ft).

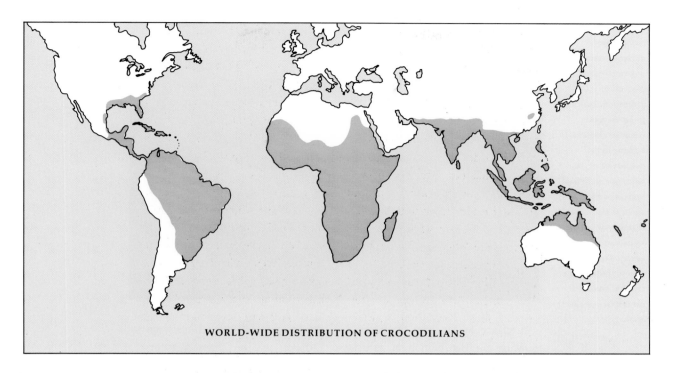

**WORLD-WIDE DISTRIBUTION OF CROCODILIANS**

continents began to form. It is thought that, prior to that break-up, crocodilians had already widely dispersed. Later, when land bridges still linked the continents of Asia and North America, the ancestral freshwater alligator line is believed to have migrated from Asia to North America, thus explaining the bizarre distribution of the Chinese and American alligators. Explanations of how the caymans, descendants of American alligator ancestors, reached South America, are still uncertain.

Recently, several investigators have suggested that the crocodilian ancestor may have also dispersed via marine migration. For this theory to hold true, the ancestral crocodilian must have had some physiological adaptation in order to survive in an aquatic environment three times as salty as its own internal fluids. This required the presence of salt-secreting glands, and, indeed, two species of modern crocodiles, the Indo-pacific saltie (*Crocodylus porosus*) and the American (*C. acutus*), are considered estuarine species. Both are known to travel considerable distances over ocean waters. The Nile crocodile (*C. niloticus*) is also able to navigate oceans to a slightly lesser degree. Indeed, seven of the 11 existing members of the Crocodylinae have salt glands in their mouths and, to varying degrees, have some capacity for oceanic dispersal.

During the Miocene period, global warming led to marked adaptive radiation of the various genera and the evolution of species of crocodilians that bore more resemblance to the modern forms. During the subsequent Pliocene period, climatic disruptions and fluctuations in sea levels led to marked changes in crocodilian distribution and the disappearance of many species known today only by their fossils.

RIGHT: Young
crocodilians
organize themselves
in groups called
crèches for
protection. This
group of young
common caymans is
basking in the
noonday sun. They
will disperse to feed
and come together
again at night. Note
that they are all the
same size; such size
segregation is
common since larger
crocodilians often
cannibalize smaller
animals.

A glance at the map on page 23 showing the distribution of existing crocodilian species within the tropical and subtropical areas of the world leads to the inescapable conclusion that their divergence is strictly limited by temperature. Although other reptiles can exist in colder climates, the northern limit of the crocodilians, seen in the Alligatorinae, is still below 34°N latitude.

## TEMPERATURE REGULATION

All crocodilians are poikilothermic – that is to say, they are cold-blooded. Unlike birds and mammals, they are incapable of shivering to generate heat and lack sweat glands necessary for evaporative cooling when the temperature gets too high. This inability to regulate the core temperature, the temperature of the brain, heart, lungs and other vital internal organs, has limited their distribution to tropical and subtropical areas, although two species,

the American alligator (*Alligator mississippiensis*) and the Chinese alligator (*A. sinensis*), have northern limits in temperate areas where they are occasionally exposed to freezing temperatures. Heat is gained from or lost to the environment in four ways: radiation; convection; conduction; and evaporative cooling. The cold-blooded crocodilians use all four methods, utilizing a complex series of physiological and behavioural mechanisms to maintain an even body temperature.

The main method of temperature regulation is through behavioural changes which involve alternating heat-seeking and heat-avoiding strategies. When their body temperature drops, they use solar radiation to heat their bodies as they emerge from the water to bask in shallow waters or on the shoreline. As their temperature rises they hold their mouths agape to allow some evaporative cooling. In reality the insides of their mouths are external surfaces in as close touch with the environment as their sensor-laden armoured skin. Thus, the membranes of the mouth cavity with their extensive blood supply play a major role in regulating both temperature and salt/water balance. If temperatures continue to rise some species adjust by seeking shade or by returning to the water. The thermal properties of water are such that it acts as a heat sink by retaining heat even when air temperatures drop.

Actually, the spectrum of behaviours used in temperature regulation are exquisitely complex. Crocodilians constantly 'ad-lib', sometimes placing a leg or tip of the nose in the sun while the rest of the body is in the shade, or orienting themselves in such a way as to minimize the absorption of the sun's rays. At other times they simultaneously partially bask in the sun while making finicky arrangements of feet, tail or head in the water. Such behaviour allows them to adjust their temperature in an optimal fashion.

Crocodilian body temperatures are also adjusted by shunting blood towards or away from their surface. As crocodilians cool, the superficial blood vessels constrict, thereby limiting the amount of heat loss at the animal's surface and maintaining a steady core temperature. Their body temperatures can also vary with activity. After feeding, some species have been observed to seek heat. The increased body temperature in turn increases the rate at which digestion occurs. On the other hand, as the environmental temperatures drop, crocodilians become progressively more lethargic. Although they do not hibernate, they do become relatively dormant. In the range of the two temperate-dwelling species of alli-

*LEFT:* Crocodilians use mud bathing to maintain their body temperature; the mud offers them a layer of insulation.

gators (*A. mississippiensis* and *A. sinensis*), cold spells occur for brief periods of time and temporary ice layers may even form on the water's surface. When this happens the animals completely submerge themselves in the deeper, warmer water, maintaining a breathing hole in the ice for their nostrils. During such times the core temperatures of the alligators can drop to as low as 5°C (41°F).

Other temperature-regulating strategies include mud bathing, which provides another layer of insulation, and burrowing into dens. Several different species excavate burrows or dens along river banks, and these dens are frequently shared by large numbers of juveniles stacked one upon another. Dens also provide a haven from predators. It has also been reported that animals suffering an infection exhibit heat-seeking behaviours to create a behavioural fever which increases their ability to fight that infection.

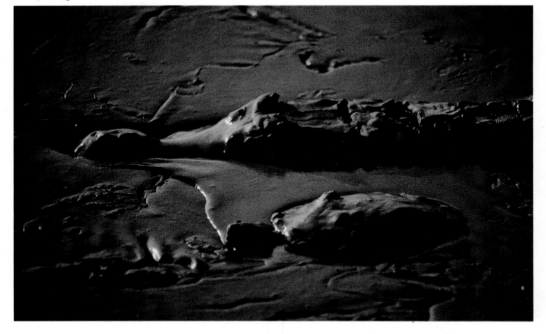

*LEFT:* Turtles and crocodilians may ignore each other, prey on one another or even compete for food. Many young alligators are eaten by large predatory turtles and some turtles end up being eaten by adult crocodilians. Here a turtle and a common cayman compete to scavenge a dead fish. Neither seems put off by the mud, which is a favourite environment for crocodilians.

# REGULATING SALTWATER BALANCE

Most modern crocodilians are freshwater inhabitants, but two species, the American crocodile (*Crocodylus acutus*) and the Indopacific crocodile (*C. porosus*), have specialized so that they are able to spend a considerable amount of time in saltwater estuaries. Although they are not considered marine or pelagic animals, they have been sighted far out at sea and have travelled hundreds of miles across the ocean to reach some isolated volcanic islands. Two other crocodiles, the Nile crocodile (*C. niloticus*) and Johnston's crocodile (*C. johnsoni*), have coastal populations that are estuarine and are known to disperse across oceanic waters to islands quite distant from the mainland shore. However, none of these estuarine species ever produces young in salt water.

All animals, freshwater, marine and terrestrial, have body fluids that are only about one-third as salty as sea water. The relative salinity and water content of the body fluids in all animals are regulated within fairly narrow limits by a variety of physiological mechanisms, a process referred to as homeostasis. Both the Archbishop of Canterbury and all crocodilians are about 70% water, but crocodiles, particularly the Indopacific, can tolerate greater fluctuations than can humans.

On land, water is primarily lost from the skin lining the crocodilian's mouth, from the moist membranes of the lung, and from the skin, particularly in the head region. Water loss in basking crocodiles is due to surface evaporation and increases as the temperature rises. Large animals with a low surface-to-volume ratio lose less water than hatchlings or juveniles. Some water is also lost via the cloaca as stool and urine.

Among those species of crocodiles that spend some time in salt water, regulating a balanced salt (mainly sodium salts) concentration is essential, particularly since sodium salts are frequently taken in during eating, a process called

ABOVE: Despite their lack of regulating salt glands, American alligators occasionally venture into salty river inlets.

BELOW: An American alligator beside a hole it has excavated in the Everglades, Florida, during the dry season.

incidental drinking. Many higher animals have highly efficient kidneys under hormonal control which regulate the relative salinity of the blood, but crocodiles have rather inefficient kidneys, and their role is mainly excretion of nitrogenous wastes. Instead, saltwater crocodiles have evolved modified salivary glands in their tongues. These glands, by expending metabolic energy, can literally pump sodium ions from the blood into the glands, which then secrete the salt. Even several freshwater, inland-dwelling crocodiles have salt glands in their tongues which may function to maintain saltwater balance during times of seasonal drought.

Neither the alligators nor their cousins the caymans have such salt glands. These animals are intolerant of salt water, although the American alligator (*Alligator mississippiensis*) occasionally makes forays into salty river inlets.

## CROCODILIAN BRAIN AND BEHAVIOUR

Crocodiles and alligators as adults have relative brain sizes that are less than 0.005% of the body weight of a 113-kg (250-lb) specimen, whereas in a human of equal size the relative weight of brain to body is a hundred times greater. This small, slowly metabolizing brain has the advantage of allowing the crocodilian to stay submerged for hours at a time. Despite the relatively small brain, crocodilians have evolved a complex repertoire of behaviours more advanced than that of any other group of reptiles. In general, the complexity of behaviour is a reflection of neural organization in the brain, particularly in ritualized

behaviours that communicate signals to do with either preservation of the individual (feeding, territoriality, co-operation, socialization, etc.) or of the species (courtship, mating, nest building, care of the young, etc.).

Only recently have scientists begun to gain insight into the complexities of crocodilian behaviour. Those aspects of species-specific communication and behavioural repertoires to do with reproduction are discussed in detail in Chapter 4 and only briefly described here.

Crocodilians use visual, auditory, chemical and vibrational signals to communicate with one another. Sometimes communication is limited to a single sensory event, but more often than not an array of signals involving two or more sensory channels is used. Some auditory communication signals are genetically programmed and express themselves during the later stages of development just prior to hatching. These sounds heard by other prehatchlings are thought to communicate hatching times and may accelerate development. In any case most of the porcelain-like eggs yield their contents more or less simultaneously, strongly suggesting hearing-related hatching times. The calls of the prehatchlings in the egg are also heard by their mother who immediately begins to dig into the nest to free the hatchlings. Once hatched, the newborn crocodilians have an alarm call that evokes aggressive protective behaviour by the nearby mother or father or both. The whine-grunt emitted by the young has been imitated by crocodile and alligator hunters to lure adults into range. Adults hearing this sound suddenly grow alert and tense and move towards the sound at speed. The distress call of the young evokes fierce aggressive behaviour on the part of the adults, who will glare at the source of the threat malevolently, hiss noisily and sometimes go into a full attack mode, charging at the intruder.

The charge of the adult is an awesome spectacle. Churning hard with its tail, it bursts out of the water mouth agape and growling loudly. There is absolutely no doubt about its intention to protect its young. But these sounds are only part of its auditory communications repertoire. In some species males generate subsonic vibrations that are conducted under water over considerable distances. Recent discoveries about sound communication have shown that a number of other animals generate low-frequency sounds below the range of human hearing. To generate these sounds, the male crocodilians lift their heads and tails out of the water, inflate their bodies and vibrate them so violently that the water over their backs

*BELOW:* In addition to audible signals – growls, roars, grunts, bellows, jaw clamps and head slaps – crocodilians also communicate by generating subaudible vibrations (sounds below the hearing level of humans). When generating subaudible vibrations they tense their bodies and vibrate their muscles, causing the water above their trunk to 'dance'.

dances like an effervescent fountain of upside-down rain. These subsonic vibrations may play a role in announcing territoriality, dominance or sexual interest. Whatever the role of these low-frequency signals, they evoke similar signalling by other nearby males.

Often the 'water dance' is followed by a thunderous roar or bellow, which in turn is followed by an almost simultaneous head slap and jaw snap as the animal drives its head into the water. This bellowing is frequently imitated by nearby males, and soon the cacophony of thunderous sound fills the air. Females read these sounds, and they too begin to bellow in rhythm. In the not-too-recent past, when thousands of crocodilians were packed along the shores, the sound of their choruses must have been awesome. Clearly, these bellows, head slaps and jaw snaps have some role in courtship and mating, but cracking the sound code of crocodilians is difficult. Unlike warm-blooded animals, their responses are slow and often delayed, so it is hard to establish stimulus-response relationships. Whatever the signalling means, it is clearly very subtle and often accompanied by visual displays and the release of chemical messengers that clarify the auditory signals.

Crocodilians have glands in their mouths and cloacas which secrete an oily, musky odorant. The sweet scent of this odorant is detectable even to the human nose. In fact some commercial crocodile farms and ranches harvest the musk glands of their slaughtered livestock to sell to perfume-makers. The musk is secreted at the time of bellowing and head-slapping and forms a

greenish sheen on the surface of the water, exactly at the level of the nostrils. The bouquet of the musk may serve as a sexual stimulant or simply announce the presence and intent of the secretor. The odorant cannot be smelled by submerged crocodilians since their nostrils are tightly closed when under water, but it may also be tasted. In all probability sound and odour are just part of an array of signals used by crocodilians. The more communication channels used, the clearer the message, as with repetition the message becomes less and less ambiguous.

Clearly, crocodilian body postures provide ample visual messages such as submissiveness, dominance, sexual interest, recognition, territoriality and status. These body postures include head-lifting, mouth-opening, submerging and blowing bubbles out of the nostrils, and subtle positionings of the body. Visual signals by females during courtship short-circuit the normal aggressive behaviour of the larger males and transform it into a desire to court and mate. The visual signals are followed by a variety of tactile signals, such as touching and pressing, that range

from the very subtle and gentle to blatant and forceful. Often during mating a variety of signals are communicated in a predictable sequence, with different species performing variations on a basic theme. The details of courtship and mating communication are discussed in more detail in Chapter 4.

## THE CROCODILIAN SENSES

The evolution of nostrils at the end of a long snout that could remain at the surface while most of the rest of the animal was submerged suggests a parallel evolution of a highly developed sense of smell. Certainly, there is within the crocodilian brain a considerable portion dedicated to olfactory perception which evokes both approach and avoidance behaviours. Odour-sensing may play a role in food location as is suggested by one example of crocodiles coming from as far away as 3 km (2 miles) to feed cooperatively on a large animal carcass. There is also substantial evidence to suggest that crocodilians use musk-like secretions as a means of communication.

to see better in dim light. Like other nocturnal hunting animals, crocodilians have a well-developed reflective surface behind the light sensors in their retinas. This structure, called the *tapetum lucidum* (L. bright carpet) contains highly reflective guanine crystals. At night, when light is reflected from the tapetum through the dilated pupils, the eyes glow eerily. One way of conducting a population census of crocodiles in a given location is to go out at night with a spotlight and count the number of yellow-orange reflecting eyes. Unfortunately, these glowing eyes also allow hunters to find them.

Some species see quite well under water while others do not orient very well when submerged. When crocodilians submerge, a contractile inner lid that is largely transparent covers the surface of the eye. Their range of vision is considerable, and predatory species such as the Indopacific crocodile (*Crocodylus porosus*) are able to spot their prey on the shore from more than 90 m (100 yd) away. They then submerge completely and move underwater directly towards their target. Starting their charge from underwater, they burst out of the water suddenly, mouths agape, and grasp their astonished prey. If you are at the water's edge and see a big crocodile well out in the water suddenly disappear, it is time to move away.

Crocodiles deprived of the sense of sight go into a hypnotic, trance-like state, a characteristic used by alligator and crocodile wrestlers to subdue large animals. A number of other animals also show this trance-like behaviour on visual disorientation, a phenomenon

Unfortunately, the size, strength and disposition of crocodilians militates against their use in sensory physiology laboratories, and not much is known about their chemical sensory perception.

Crocodilians are also very visually oriented animals. The eyes, located high and laterally on the dorsal surface of the head, project above the surface when most of the remainder of the animal is submerged. The eyes are relatively large and have motile upper and lower lids that, at rest, are partially closed, giving the animal a mellow, sleepy look. In bright light the pupils reflexively close, limiting the amount of light reaching the retina and presenting a vertical, slit-like appearance, but in the dark the pupils open dramatically. The eyes fit into bony orbits in the skull and, if pressed upon, sink into the orbit and no longer project. The retina contains both rods and cones, the latter for acute colour vision. Crocodilians' eyes have a considerably larger number of rods than do human eyes, allowing them

*ABOVE:* One reason adult crocodilians are virtually invulnerable is their awesome armoured skin, the structure of which is very obvious in this basking American alligator.

known as tonic immobility. It is not only seen in many cold-blooded amphibians and reptiles but also in birds and mammals such as rabbits.

Given the array of sounds and the spectrum of acoustically evoked behaviours, it is clear that crocodilians have an exquisite sense of hearing. On a line with and directly behind the eyes are the slit-like openings to the external ears. Each ear opening is protected by a muscular flap which acts like a water-limiting valve when the animal submerges. Unlike the mammalian ear, which has an arrangement of three tiny bones to amplify sound from the eardrum to the inner ear, crocodilians have only a single, very thin bone. How well they hear underwater is not known, but sound is conducted better in water than in air, and some of their behaviour patterns suggest that they do detect underwater sound. The fact that crocodilians have their three main senses, smell, sight and sound, all on-line even when most of their body is submerged, indicates how intimately they are in contact with their external environment.

## CROCODILIAN SKIN

The evolution of dorsal armour in the skin of ancestral crocodilians is apparent as early as the late Triassic period in the fossil remains of the early proto-suchians. The function of this early armour is not clear; it may have been defensive or it may have given additional support to the backbone when they came ashore and walked. Modern crocodilians, for the most part, retain some dorsal armour, and its extent varies with species. Most modern species have significantly reduced dorsal neck armour,

an adaptation that has permitted greater flexibility and range of head movements that are so much a part of the crocodilian behavioural repertoire.

Crocodilian skin, in all 22 species, is made of tough, leathery scales set in a flat pavement fashion. Some scales are joined at their edges by a more elastic skin. Usually each scale is clearly a separate entity, but in some parts of the body they do overlap. The skin on the head is fused directly to the bony skull, and in some species the skin on the dorsal part of the neck forms a shield composed of large, ridged projections. Embedded in the skin's scales are tough, horny, plate-like structures called scutes, and below the scutes on the back and tail are pitted, bony plates or ostea. On the dorsal side the scales form sharply keeled double rows that fuse into a single row about midway along the tail. The scales on the lower sides and on the ventral or belly surface are usually unarmoured, and it is this unfortunate lack of ventral armour that has pushed most of the 22 species to the edge of extinction.

Once it was discovered that crocodilian skin made a fine, handsome leather, commercialization of their skins became a highly profitable enterprise. Their fate was sealed. All the generalist adaptations that had withstood 200 million years of survival pressure came to naught as opulent consumers opted to wear and carry status symbols of their wealth made of crocodile hides. It was not just the quality of the leather that made them attractive but also the skins' handsome geometric patterns. The 'skins game' is examined in some depth in Chapter 6.

ONE

—

# CROCODILES
# IN
# MYTH,
# RELIGION
# AND
# ART

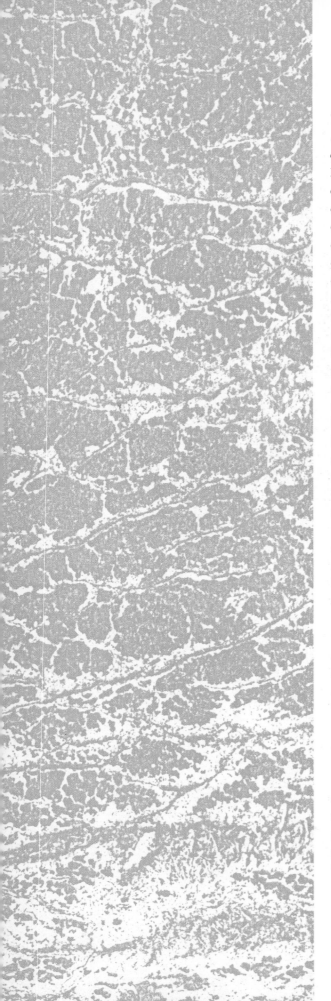

From the time of the earliest peoples, the destinies of humans and crocodilians have become inextricably linked. Both early humans and crocodilians required water and a semitropical or tropical climate. Although there is no record of their interactions in prehistoric times, crocodile teeth have sometimes been included in very ancient grave sites. Studies of modern primitive peoples certainly include many mentions of crocodilians in their creation myths, which may be thousands of years old, and in many of these cultures crocodile hunting is well documented. However, given the size and strength of an adult crocodile and its stealthy, efficient and opportunistic feeding behaviour, untold thousands of humans must have fallen prey to their appetites over the years. It is not surprising, therefore, that many ancient peoples viewed crocodiles with a mixture of fear, hate and loathing.

Probably the most familiar expression of crocodilophobia is found in the biblical discussion of Leviathan as a symbolic villain (*Job* 41:1; and *Psalms* 74:14), to be overcome by belief in God:

*'Who can open the doors to his face?*
*His teeth are terrible round about. His*
*scales are his pride shut up together*
*as with a closed seal. One is so*
*near to another, that no air can*
*come between them . . . His eyes*
*are like the eyelids of morning.'*

The lattermost phrase was used by Alistair Graham and Peter Beard as the title of their somewhat bizarre but compelling book about the Nile crocodiles (*Crocodylus niloticus*) of the Jade Sea (Lake Turkana, Kenya). What emerges from their book is that the Nile crocodile was found as far north along the shores of the Mediterranean as Syria and present-day Israel as recently as 100 years ago. Clearly, the interactions of the Ancient Hebrews and Nile crocodiles led to their inclusion in the scriptures. Similar inclusions of crocodiles into religious myth are found in many different faiths, but none exceeded those of the Egyptians.

The deification of the crocodile probably had its origins in sheer terror of the fearsome, powerful beasts that preyed upon both people and cattle. Then, as now, the majority of the population of Egypt dwelt along the banks of the River Nile, which was very densely populated by Nile crocodiles. Such terrible gods needed to be placated and, according to the reports of such ancient historians as Herodotus, in Egypt this placation of the river god consisted of the annual sacrifice of a virgin thrown into the Nile with pomp and ceremony. However, a precautionary word about the reports of these early writers of history. Catherine Bard, a professor of archaeology of early Egypt, wrote: 'Such reports when viewed critically must be taken with considerable scepticism.' Nevertheless, it is clear that by 2400 BC a well-documented crocodile god had emerged. This god, Sobek (Sebek, Sebek-Ra), had the head of a crocodile and the body of a man.

The temple of the crocodile god, Kom Ombo, is located 48 km (30 miles) south of Edfu on a bend of the Nile. This stately temple, now in a state of considerable disrepair, is dedicated to Sobek and another deity, the falcon-headed Horus. The temple was built in the time of the Ptolemies, and the Greek influence is strong. By the fifth century BC decadence had set

*ABOVE:* Statue of the Egyptian god Sobek with Pharaoh Amenhotep III, which can be seen in the Luxor Museum in Egypt. Sobek was always depicted with a crocodile's head and a man's body.

in and other animal cults emerged that placed their particular deities (there were over 400 Egyptian gods) in a position of dominance. Under the Greek influence the crocodile god was called Souchos. At Kom Ombo and at the temples in Crocodilopolis, the centre of crocodile worship, crocodiles were kept in ponds, ministered to by priests, adorned with jewellery and fed regularly. Some of the sacred crocodiles were quite tame, and priests would hand-feed them with meat, cakes, bread and honey. The poor beasts must have been quite plump and lethargic. When they died, their bodies were embalmed, then wrapped for mummification and stored in large vaults. Today tourists visiting these sites can see the vaults piled floor-to-ceiling with hundreds of crocodile mummies.

The images of the crocodile god varied depending on the period in Egyptian art. Sometimes the crocodile-headed man wore either a solar disk encircled with a *uraeus* (a band of cobras signifying royal rank) or had a pair of horns supporting a solar disk and a pair of large plumes. At other times Sobek was simply depicted as a crocodile. In pre-dynastic times Sobek was probably the representative of Evil, but later he was identified with the sun god Ra and was called Sobek-Ra. It is beyond the scope of this book to go into the complex and elaborate discussion of the place of Sobek in Egyptian religion, and the reader wishing to delve deeper can consult any scholarly text on Egyptology. What is surprising is that in a recent Walt Disney comic book, *The Crocodile Collector*, the whole theme consists of

Donald Duck seeking out the lost temple of Sobek.

Not only did the Nile crocodile serve as an object of religious veneration in Egypt, but other peoples also developed similar forms of worship. The Buganda people of present-day Uganda built a crocodile temple on an island in crocodile-infested Lake Victoria, and on its shores enemies (with arms and legs broken) were offered up in sacrifice to placate the fearsome, toothsome deity. The Bobo tribe of Upper Volta also practised human sacrifice to Nile crocodiles.

In cultures from South-east Asia to Australia, legends, folk tales, totemism, creation myths and morality stories have been woven into quasi-religious myths. Sometimes crocodiles were used as tools by gods and sorcerers, serving as avenging spirits sent to bring retribution to those guilty of some misdeed. The idea of placating gods by human sacrifice was not only practised in Africa but also in Indonesia, often involving the sacrifice of young maidens. Such practices were considered to be the highest form of placation, for symbolically these hapless young women were to become wives of the terrible, malevolent denizens of the waters. Frequently, primitive religions included taboos about killing crocodiles; thus, the

*LEFT AND FACING PAGE:* In China, ivory was a preferred medium for decorative carvings. It is ironic that the product of one endangered species, the elephant, is used to depict the demise of another endangered species, the crocodile.

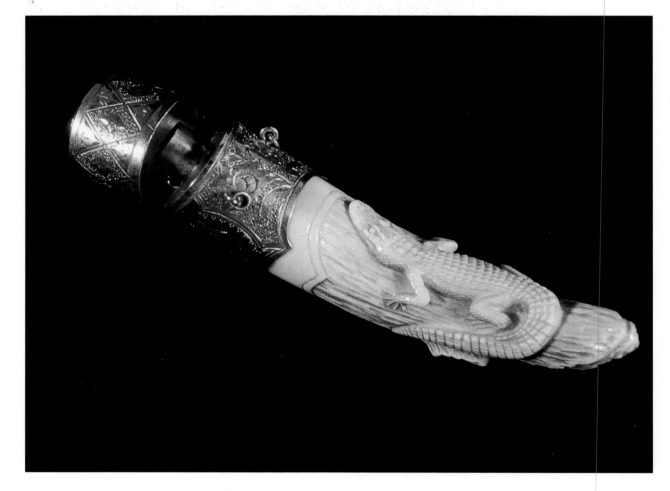

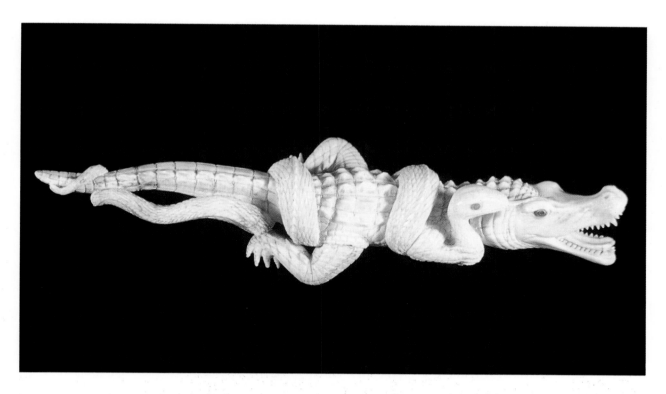

Dyaks of Borneo and the Nuer people of the Upper Nile forbade crocodile hunting. In other places the taboo limited crocodile hunting to a reciprocal relationship, and only when a family member was killed by a crocodile could the grieving survivors collect their payback by killing a crocodile. Elsewhere, in a variation of the Middle Ages test of trial by ordeal, someone accused of a crime would have to cross a crocodile-infested river. Supposedly by divine inspiration the crocodiles could differentiate between the guilty and the innocent and so a successful crossing proved the accused's virtue.

The decorative arts of a culture reflect motifs, times, symbols and patterns that often go back to the most remote epochs of human experience. They are expressed in traditional designs and also represent the technology available to the artists, artisans and craftsmen of that period.

Some of the *objets d'art* were used for personal adornment, some for ceremonial ritual purposes, some for religious ceremonial expressions and some for decorative ornamentation of the home. These renderings included sculptures and carvings in wood, bronze and ivory, tapestries, weavings and paintings. The richness and diversity of the artisans' creations reflecting the crocodilian impact on the human

*BELOW:* Among the Ashanti tribe of Ghana, the Nile crocodile was an object of fear and admiration which was incorporated into their tribal arts.

psyche can be seen in some of the objects described in this chapter. Of course this section on crocodilian art is not intended to be exhaustive.

Probably the oldest representation of a crocodile dates back about 30,000 years to an early Australian aboriginal stone engraving showing a remarkably correct crocodile head.

With the discovery of the Americas, European artists had a heyday depicting the images brought back by the early explorers. These invariably involved a rather voluptuous native woman dressed in feathers and usually mounted on an alligator or crocodile and all entitled 'America'. Clearly the emblem of savagery was both the native Indian and the crocodilian. These images were carved in marble, baked as porcelains and painted on walls and ceilings. The crocodilian, the appropriate denizen of these waterbound continents, was always presented as the constant companion of a human female. One magnificent porcelain by Meissen (1745) shows an alligator with a raised, mobile tongue, clearly an anatomical error. Giovani Battista Tiepolo's 1753 version and Wolfgang Baumgartner's (1750–60) paintings of America were dominated by crocodiles, and the charms of America were given exotic qualities. In each *objet d'art* the illusion of the crocodilian bore only a superficial resemblance to the real animal, as did the work of many primitive artisans of the past (and even the present day).

Each year thousands of Moslem pilgrims trek to the famous 'Mugger Pit' in Karachi, Pakistan, to visit a few dozen obese, sacred mugger crocodiles (*Crocodylus palustris*). These animals traditionally were regarded as sacred and often had verses of the Koran painted on their heads. The pilgrims thronged along the dusty tracks to offer placation to these

*ABOVE:* In the marketplaces of Central American countries such as El Salvador, crocodile carvings are relatively common. The local artists feel free to use designs and colours not found in living crocodiles.

*BELOW:* In ancient Mexico the rivers abounded with the American crocodile, Morelet's crocodile and caymans. Stories of them were recorded in folklore and immortalized in carvings and ceramics.

*FACING PAGE, BELOW:* With the discovery of the Americas, artists in Europe became fascinated with the stories brought back by explorers and made them the subject of their artistic endeavors. This porcelain piece depicts the maiden America as a robust native woman with a feather headdress, bow and arrow sitting astride a rather unreal giant alligator.

feared beasts, which were fed and attended
to by religious men. Today, it is primarily
a tourist attraction, but there remains
some residue of the old animalistic
ceremonies.

Another myth from the Indian sub-
continent describes a legendary battle
between a crocodile and an elephant.
According to legend, the Hindu god
Krishna comes to the elephant's aid. It
was this legend that led Rudyard Kipling
to write his short story *The Elephant's
Child*.

In Ghana, among the Ashanti Tribe, the
crocodile is represented both in bronze
and wooden carvings. The bronzes are
particularly interesting because of the use
of the lost wax method in making the
castings. One ritual funerary urn has four
human figures on the cover, one firmly
locked in the jaws of a Nile crocodile.
Another figure tries to spear the offending

beast while two nearby female figures wail in grief. The Ashanti traditional style of depicting crocodiles hasn't varied over the years, and modern castings and carvings dutifully follow the design. In Central America the artists took considerably greater licence in their portrayal of crocodiles in wood and ceramics. Some are quite dramatically coloured and in no way attempt to present a realistic image, yet there is no question that these are crocodiles.

In modern times the crocodile has appeared in popular culture in a variety of bizarre ways. The alligator has also been adopted by the Lacoste Company, and large numbers of students and young professionals stroll about in brightly coloured tennis shirts adorned with a grinning crocodile logo. Even popular slang in some countries has turned reptilian: 'See you later, Alligator' merits the ritual response 'After a while, Crocodile.'

In the popular culture of the cinema crocodilians are usually depicted in an evil light. Those readers old enough will vividly recall the early African adventure movies such as *Trader Horn* and *Frank Buck – Bring 'Em Back Alive* which showed hordes of giant crocodiles slipping

malevolently into the water from their basking sites. Buck was notorious for creating scenes and situations with captured animals, and in one film he staged a battle between a python and a small crocodile (the python won). But the ultimate crocodile movie is Paramount Pictures' *Crocodile Dundee*, in which the hero is actually a part-time poacher endowed with unusual skills. When the heroine is almost pulled into a billabong by a large saltwater crocodile, Mick Dundee dispatches the offending beast with his knife – hardly true to life but compelling viewing. The Disney Studio has frequently used animated cartoon crocodiles pictured in both benign and malign roles such as the corps de ballet of smiling crocodiles in *Fantasia* and the ticking 'croc who swallowed the clock' in *Peter Pan*.

The ambivalence of humans towards crocodilians is also reflected in many children's books. Some authors portray crocodiles and alligators as charming, sweet, smiling and benign creatures. This is potentially harmful as in reality large crocodilians are powerful, unpredictable and dangerous animals. Sometimes a healthy respect is called for, as there have been instances of people being attacked while trying to feed animals in parks. Perhaps the lyrics of the little song *Never Smile at a Crocodile* present a true cautionary message.

**ABOVE:** An Ashanti funerary urn made in bronze. The figures on the lid show a man firmly grasped in the jaws of a large crocodile while another man tries to spear the offending predator and two villagers express their grief.

**RIGHT:** In Papua New Guinea, crocodiles were often the subject of artistic expression such as the carving on the prow of this local war canoe.

**ABOVE RIGHT:** This Mexican wooden carving, while not anatomically accurate, is still clearly a crocodile.

# TWO

# THE
# EVOLUTION
# OF
# THE
# CROCODILIANS

In Rudyard Kipling's story *The Elephant's Child*, Kipling explains how the crocodile played a role in providing elephants with their trunks. In this very un-Darwinian tale, everything occurs 'In the High and Far Off Times' when primitive elephants had no trunks, only 'a blackish, bulgy nose, as big as a boot'. There was, however, one 'satiably curious Elephant's Child' who wished to know what the crocodile had for dinner. The Elephant's Child at last arrived at the banks of '. . . the great, grey-green greasy Limpopo River, all set about with fever trees' and found the crocodile. 'Come hither, Little One,' said the crocodile, and as he spoke 'he wept crocodile tears' to show his sincerity. Suddenly the crocodile caught the Elephant's Child's nose with his 'musky, tusky mouth'. The Elephant's Child sat back on his haunches and pulled and pulled, and the crocodile in the water 'with great sweeps of his tail' tried to pull the little elephant into the water. The Elephant's Child's nose kept on stretching, and at last, when the crocodile let go, the nose stayed stretched. And that's how elephants got their trunks.

Our understanding of crocodilian evolution, while not as whimsical as Kipling's, is nonetheless as fascinating and far better documented. During the Age of Reptiles or Mesozoic era, a great variety of reptiles evolved and dominated the Earth for more than 100 million years. Of these, one major group, the ruling reptiles or dinosaurs, diversified, giving rise to a large variety of now-extinct forms as well as the only current-day survivors, the birds and the crocodilians.

From the ancestral dinosaurs during the first period (Triassic) of the Mesozoic era evolved an ancient group of animals called Thecodontia. Like the modern crocodilians, these thecodonts had sharp, pointed teeth set in bony sockets of the lower and upper jaws. Most were small and had long hind legs and short forelegs. Many of these reptiles evolved a bipedal gait, which gave them a considerable speed advantage, given the longer hind legs. Some, however, reverted to a four-legged gait, still retaining, nonetheless, shorter forelegs, a condition seen in all crocodilians. Some of these reptiles also developed rows of bony plates in their skin; this armour-plating was retained, to varying degrees, in both ancient and modern crocodilians. The increased weight of armour encouraged some of these ancestral thecodonts to take to the water, where the weight was compensated for by buoyancy. Of these early water-dwellers, some became exclusively aquatic, while others became amphibious forms that frequented the banks of rivers, lakes and estuaries.

All of these aquatic predators were air-breathers that, over time, developed several adaptations permitting them to stay submerged for long periods. Those forms that hunted along the shores for land-dwellers coming to drink exhibited another evolutionary strategy: the ability to submerge most of the body while leaving the air-breathing tube and eyes just above the waterline. Thus, these armoured snorkellers became adept at hiding themselves at the water's edge. In developing their snorkelling strategy the early ancestors of the crocodilians located their breathing apparatus on top of their heads between their eyes. This provided them with a direct, short air passageway to the lungs; however, it also deprived them of an important sensory system: because their nostrils were submerged, they could

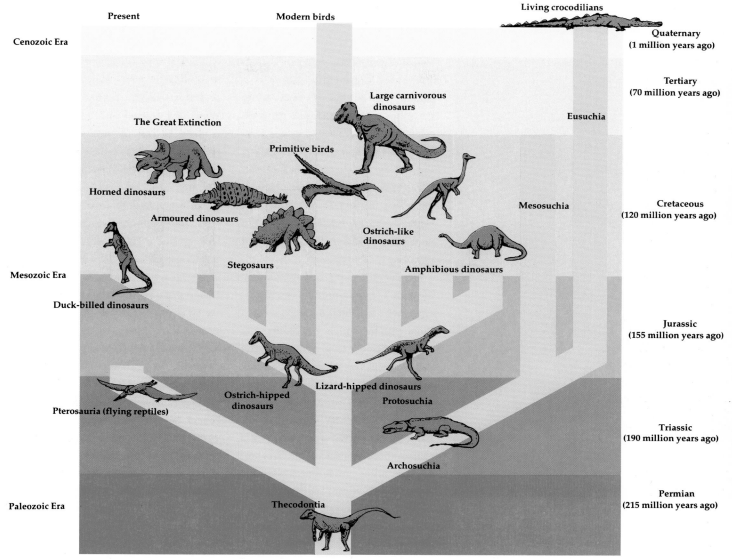

Present      Modern birds      Living crocodilians

Cenozoic Era

**Quaternary**
**(1 million years ago)**

**Tertiary**
**(70 million years ago)**

Large carnivorous dinosaurs

The Great Extinction

Eusuchia

Primitive birds

Horned dinosaurs

Armoured dinosaurs

Mesosuchia

Ostrich-like dinosaurs

**Cretaceous**
**(120 million years ago)**

Stegosaurs

Amphibious dinosaurs

Mesozoic Era

Duck-billed dinosaurs

**Jurassic**
**(155 million years ago)**

Lizard-hipped dinosaurs

Protosuchia

Ostrich-hipped dinosaurs

Pterosauria (flying reptiles)

**Triassic**
**(190 million years ago)**

Archosuchia

**Permian**
**(215 million years ago)**

Paleozoic Era

Thecodontia

Stem of ruling reptiles

**THE EVOLUTIONARY TIMESCALE**

*ABOVE:* The geologic periods, their duration and the dominant life forms of the various periods are shown in this table. Note that the protosuchian ancestors of the true crocodiles, the Eusuchia, date back to 190–200 million years. While all other descendants of the ruling reptiles were wiped out during the great extinctions at the Cretaceous/Tertiary Boundary, the crocodiles and their distant cousins, the modern birds, flourished.

not use smell to locate prey. This design defect was corrected early in the history of the crocodilians by moving the opening of the breathing apparatus, the nostrils, to the front of the long snout. Thus, crocodilians had the advantage of being able to submerge almost all of their bodies, exposing only the tops of their heads, while still having full use of all three sensory systems, visual, auditory and olfactory.

While the fossil record of the ancestral crocodilians is not complete, it is still possible to construct a reasonably good

history of crocodilian evolution. The success of their evolutionary adaptations is attested by the fact that they alone, among the ruling reptiles, survived the great extinctions that occurred 65 million years ago at the Cretaceous-Tertiary boundary, and that the basic crocodilian form was fully developed by the Jurassic period. (Note that the Jurassic period occurred between about 200 million and 135 million years ago, following the Triassic and preceding the Cretaceous periods.)

Some of these changes could be seen in the early (215 million years ago) small, armoured, long-limbed, short-snouted Proto (before)-suchia (crocodiles), in which the first development of a secondary palate of bone that separated the air passageway from the roof of the mouth could be seen.

At the time of the Protosuchia the Earth's landmass was a single structure, a supercontinent known as Pangea. Thus, dispersal of the protosuchians was easy. As the supercontinent split and portions

of it moved apart, a phenomenon known as continental drift, the protosuchian populations became isolated from each other, and evolved and diversified in response to varying natural selection pressures. The first of these specialized crocodilians were the Meso (mid)-suchia. The Mesosuchia left a considerable fossil record dating back to about 190 million years ago. These long-snouted crocodilians evolved a highly conspicuous and fully developed false palate made of bone. This structure or partition ran the entire length of the mouth, thereby separating the air passages from the throat. At the internal end of the airway, the throat and air passageway were separated by a muscular flap, a valve-like structure that allowed the crocodilian to breathe with its mouth open while submerged. (It should be noted that water leaks into crocodilians' tooth-lined mouths even when their jaws are clamped shut.)

The fossil remnants of some mesosuchian crocodilians strongly indicate

*ABOVE:* One of the keys to the survival of crocodilians is their ability to submerge most of their bodies while still having full use of three senses – sight, hearing and smell.

*BELOW:* The earliest crocodiles, the Protosuchia, evolved from the ancestor of the ruling reptiles, the Thecodonts. Though long extinct we can recreate their

appearance from the fossil record. They were longer legged than modern crocodilians and had shorter snouts. Their nostrils were located

near the eyes (unlike the Eusuchia) but they did have a four-chambered heart, a diaphragm and armoured skin.

that some of them underwent structural adaptations to an aquatic or marine life. The arrangement of their teeth in long, thin snouts suggests that they, like the modern gharyal, were primarily fish-eaters. Some of the later mesosuchians became totally adapted to the marine environment. These ocean-dwellers replaced legs with paddle-like appendages, lost their armour and evolved a large dorsal fin near the end of their long, muscular tails. This fin was used like a gondolier's oar to propel them through the water. Although some of these specialized mesosuchians and metriohynchids (dolphin-like crocodilians) were successful, eventually they became extinct in the early Cretaceous period of the Mesozoic era. Other mesosuchians developed adaptations similar to those of the modern crocodiles, and they persisted from the mid-Jurassic, through the Cretaceous and into the early Tertiary.

The mesosuchians continued in a variety of diverse aquatic, amphibious and terrestrial forms into the early Cretaceous. Some evolved vertebrae and dorsal armour similar to those of the Eusuchia. All the diverse mesosuchians, however, disappeared during the time of the great extinctions. This débâcle occurred at the boundary of the Cretaceous and Tertiary periods and has been attributed to severe climatic changes brought about by either a huge meteor or asteroid colliding with the Earth, the impact of a comet on the Earth, or to an enormous surge of volcanic activity. The result of such a cataclysmic event would have been the injection of vast amounts of debris, dust, soot and ash into the atmosphere, shielding out the life-giving light of the sun and causing severe temperature changes. Among the

*ABOVE:* Some of the ancestors of modern crocodilians, the mesosuchians, evolved and adapted to a purely marine environment, as did the dolphin-like pair of geosauruses shown here.

*BELOW:* A fossilized jaw of *Gavialosuchus Americanus*. The fossil record of the gharyal is relatively complete, with examples dating back to the late Tertiary period.

*BELOW:* Primitive though they may appear, crocodilians have avoided extinction by occupying an ecological niche free from competition and major predators.

survivors were the cold-blooded true crocodilians (the eusuchians), freshwater fishes, amphibians and turtles. The fact that modern crocodilians are extremely sensitive to cold and cannot survive protracted exposure suggests that temperature change was not the critical factor in the extinction of so many marine and terrestrial forms of life.

One possible explanation is that freshwater-dwellers were neither dependent on flowering plants (the main food of terrestrial herbivores) nor marine plankton (the main food of marine herbivores). Both flowering plants and marine plankton were devastated by the cataclysmic events, whatever they were, during the period of the great extinctions. However, the survivors, the freshwater-dwellers, including many of the true crocodilians, were able to carry on because their food webs remained relatively intact. For a more comprehensive review of this aspect of crocodilian evolution, I recommend Eric Buffetaut's chapter in *Crocodiles and Alligators* (Facts on File, 1990).

The eusuchians gave rise to the modern crocodilians, although construction of an exact family tree is not without controversy. Tracing an ancestry as ancient as that of the crocodilians follows several lines of evidence. The ability to determine the age of fossils, along with fossil evidence provided by paleontologists, provides a good base. Fortunately, the crocodilians were semi-aquatic, and upon their deaths frequently became embedded in mud, hence readily fossilized. But even though they left an extensive fossil record, there are still significant gaps. Another line of evidence is based on the comparative anatomy of extinct and living eusuchians, particularly the structure of the skeletal components – especially the skulls. More recently, additional clues to crocodilian lineage are being provided by the use of comparative biochemical and molecular studies. When all these pieces of evidence are collected, a more complete (albeit still controversial) story of the history of the eusuchian emerges.

The gharyal's (*Gavialis gangeticus*) fossil history is quite complete, going back to the late Tertiary. Certain fossil evidence suggests that these long-snouted crocodilians were ancestral to the living false gharyal (*Tomistoma schlegelii*), and this evidence is supported by biochemical studies by L.D. Densmore and R.D. Owen, who believe that the gharyal and false gharyal share a common lineage. Other morphological anatomical studies, however, suggest that the false gharyal belongs to the subfamily Crocodylinae.

Of the modern eusuchians there are only three surviving subfamilies: the Gavialinae; the Crocodylinae; and the Alligatorinae. The fossil record of species in the genus *Crocodylus* is known with some precision all the way back to the early Tertiary period. This includes a number of extinct species that possibly were ancestral to the present-day crocodiles. Knowledge of the linkage of other extinct species is at best obscure. Despite these gaps in the evolutionary history of present-day crocodilians, it is clear that the basic crocodilian blueprint for survival has been successful for almost 190 million years. The key to this survival has been to keep things simple and conservative and to stick mainly to freshwater or estuarine habitats where they occupy ecological niches devoid of other large predators. Those crocodilians that tried to specialize in other habitats became extinct.

THREE

—

# A
# GUIDE
# TO
# LIVING
# CROCODILIANS

odern crocodilians enjoy a world-wide distribution, throughout the warmer parts of the world, and two species, the Chinese alligator (*Alligator sinensis*) and the American alligator (*A. mississippiensis*), have ranges that extend into temperate latitudes where, on occasion, freezing temperatures are experienced. All belong to the family Crocodylidae and probably all three subfamilies (the Crocodylinae, the Alligatorinae and the Gavialinae) evolved from a single long-nosed ancestor. It is thought that the Gavialinae were the first to arise, followed by the Crocodylinae and, probably the most recent, the Alligatorinae.

The Gavialinae consist of two long-nosed genera, *Tomistoma* and *Gavialis*, of which there is only one species in each genus. The animals have very long, rounded slender snouts, and their jaws are lined with many (80–100) even-sized, sharp-pointed, interlocking teeth.

The Crocodylinae are made up of two genera, *Crocodylus*, of which there are 12 species, and *Osteolaemus*, of which there is only one species. It should be noted that some taxonomists include the genus *Tomistoma* among this subfamily. Their snouts are generally tapered towards the front. Snout width varies with species.

They have different-sized teeth and when their jaws are closed, the teeth of the lower jaw fit into the upper jaw with the exception of the large pair of fourth teeth, which fit into a pronounced notch near the front upper jaw. This clearly visible fourth tooth and the presence of visible sensory pits on the ventral scales are the best identification markers separating the Crocodylinae from the Alligatorinae.

In the Alligatorinae there are four genera: *Melanosuchus* with only one species; *Alligator* with two species; *Paleosuchus* with two species; and *Caiman* with two species.

The following pages contain a description of each species and a summary of its current survival status. CITES I indicates that the species is endangered and CITES II that it is not endangered but possibly threatened. (CITES is the Convention on International Trade in Endangered Species, a treaty drawn up in 1973 and signed by over 80 countries.) The other organizations' classification usages are clear: either endangered or not endangered. These groupings are determined by the International Union for Conservation of Nature and Natural Resources (IUCN) and the US Endangered Species Act (ESA).

# Haryial or Gharyal
## *Gavialis gangeticus*

**Description:**

The crocodilian with the longest, narrowest snout has about 100 interlocking, even-sized, sharp-pointed teeth. Adult males have a conspicuous knob or ghar at the tip of their snouts. Light olive-tan coloured with darker blotches and bands. It is a poor walker and doesn't stray far from water, having more extensive webbing between its toes than any other crocodilian. Its neck armour is continuous with its back armour. Some specimens reach lengths of 6.4 m (21 ft), and one report in 1908 recorded a specimen measuring more than 9 m (30 ft).

**Habitat and Distribution:**

Mainly limited to broad-banked rivers of Pakistan, Bangladesh, Burma, India and Nepal.

**Status:**

Although protected by law due to heavy hunting, gill net fishing and habitat destruction, the natural populations teeter on the brink of extinction. As a result the gharyal is listed in CITES I and as 'Endangered' by IUCN and ESA. Currently being restocked from heat-started farm-reared eggs, and more reintroduction efforts are in progress, so there is some cause for optimism.

**Gharyal**

## Reproduction:

Adults slowly build deep, sandy hole nests in which 30–40 eggs are laid in two layers. The hatchlings are very large, up to 36 cm (14 in), and are grey-brown and striped on both body and tail.

**Gharyal**

**False gharyal**

# False Haryial or Gharyal
## *Tomistoma schlegelii*

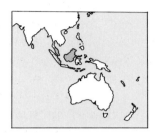

## Description:

Although listed as a member of the subfamily Crocodylinae by many experts, recent research suggests that it is probably a member of the subfamily Gavialinae. A dark-coloured animal with conspicuous black bands and blotches on its sides, tail and jaws, this species has a very long, slender snout with about 80 equally-sized, sharp-pointed teeth. Adult sizes average 3 m (9.8 ft), but individuals of 4 m (13 ft) have been recorded.

## Habitat and Distribution:

Found in freshwater swamps, lakes and rivers in the Malay Peninsula, Borneo, Sumatra and Java, although a few hundred years ago they may have ranged as far north as China.

## Status:

Severely depleted over much of its range due to habitat destruction and hunting, this species is listed in CITES I and is considered 'Endangered' by ESA and IUCN.

## Reproduction:

Very little is known about this species in its natural habitat. Some captive breeding in zoos and farms where it is a mound nester.

## Predator/Prey:

Mainly fish, but is known to take a variety of small vertebrates.

## Orinoco Crocodile
### *Crocodylus intermedius*

**Description:**

A very large species, up to 7 m (23 ft), very similar to the American crocodile (*C. acutus*), except that its dorsal armour is symmetrical and its snout is thinner. Underside light-coloured, dorsal and side plates yellow-green to tan with darker plates and stripes.

**Habitat and Distribution:**

Usually found in quiet waters of rivers and lagoons of the Orinoco River basin in eastern Colombia and Venezuela. Shares its range with the American crocodile at the mouth of the Orinoco.

**Status:**

Due to extensive hunting for its hide, this species has been decimated and the population is having problems in recovering. Less than 100 individuals are left in Venezuela. Some captive breeding is taking place in the hope of repopulating depleted areas. Although the Orinoco crocodile is protected by both Venezuela and Colombia, law enforcement is lax. Listed in CITES I and as 'Endangered' by IUCN and ESA.

**Reproduction:**

A hole nester thought to be similar in habits to the American crocodile.

**Predator/Prey:**

Thought to be primarily a fish-eater, but like most crocodilians, is opportunistic and takes birds, reptiles and mammals too.

## American Crocodile
### *Crocodylus acutus*

**Description:**

Full-grown adults are dark tan to deep olive-brown. Some have spots and bands, and their eyes are characterized by silver-grey irises. Young are yellow-tan with darker markings on body and tail. Their dorsal armour is asymmetrical. All have a typical crocodile snout and a distinct hump just between and in front of the eyes. They grow to considerable size, up to 6 m (20 ft) or more, although the average adult length of today's specimens is 3.4 m (11 ft).

**Habitat and Distribution:**

The most northern-dwelling crocodile. A population of about 500 individuals may be found in coastal lagoons, estuaries, keys, rivers, lakes and canals of extreme southern Florida, USA. Other populations are found in Cuba (where it is known to hybridize with Cuban crocodiles, *C. rhombifer*), Jamaica, Hispaniola, southern Mexico to Venezuela on the Atlantic side and on the Pacific side from southern Mexico to Ecuador and Peru. Considered an estuarine species capable of migrating through salt water.

**Orinoco crocodile**

American crocodile

## Status:

Listed as 'Endangered' by ESA and IUCN and included in the CITES I appendix, its populations have been severely depleted and continue to be so by illegal hunting despite legal protection. Habitat destruction is responsible for some of the reduction, and in inhabited areas motor vehicles are a major killer. Habitat retention plans are in place and recovery strategies planned.

## Reproduction:

A hole nester on sandy banks of rivers and canals; good parental care.

## Predator/Prey:

Large individuals eat fish, mammals, birds, turtles.

# Cuban Crocodile
## *Crocodylus rhombifer*

### Description:

A very short-snouted species with prominent bumps at the rear of its skull. The rear leg armour is ridged. Adult animals are dark with yellow spots. Of medium size – about 3 m (10 ft) in length – although in the recent past there have been reports of larger animals.

### Habitat and Distribution:

Ponds and channels of freshwater swamps in south-west Cuba and Isla de Pinos.

### Status:

Included in CITES I and listed as 'Endangered' by both IUCN and ESA, despite legal protection by the government. Shares its range and breeds with the American crocodile (*C. acutus*) and the spectacled cayman (*Caiman crocodilus*), an introduced species. The Cuban government has thousands of Cuban crocodiles breeding on farms for commercial exploitation and for possible restocking.

### Reproduction:

Not much is known about its habits in the wild; a hole nester.

### Predator/Prey:

Fish and small mammals; has a very aggressive disposition.

Cuban crocodile

# Morelet's Crocodile
## *Crocodylus moreletii*

### Description:

A small-to-medium-sized, broad-snouted species measuring 3.0–3.4 m (10–11 ft), with a raised, blunt ridge along the top of its nose. It has prominent, heavy neck scales. Its eyes bear a light-coloured iris, and adults are dark brown with black spots and stripes.

### Habitat and Distribution:

Usually found in freshwater ponds, rivers, streams and marshes, although some populations are coastal in Central America on the Atlantic side from Tamaulipas in Mexico southward to northern Guatemala.

### Status:

Although protected by law, Morelet's crocodile is poached throughout its range. Listed in CITES I as 'Endangered' by IUCN. Breeds readily; restocking planned.

Morelet's crocodile

# Nile Crocodile
## *Crocodylus niloticus*

### Description:

Although there are several subspecies of somewhat varying appearance, most Nile crocodiles are uniformly dark grey-brown with darker cross-bands on their tails, while their abdomens are generally light in colour. Adults average about 3.7 m (12 ft), but there are larger individuals, 5.5 m (18 ft) or more, in some populations. One unconfirmed turn-of-the-century account claimed a hunter killed one measuring 7.3 m (24 ft).

### Habitat and Distribution:

This once-widely distributed species ranged up the coast of the Middle East to Palestine but today is no longer found north of the fourth cataract on the Nile in Egypt. Populations also used to exist in Lake Chad in the Sahara. Still found in rivers, lakes and swamps of most of tropical Africa. A population is still present in Madagascar (the Malagasay Republic) but no longer in the Seychelle Islands. Some populations are estuarine.

### Status:

Some populations are listed as 'Endangered', others as 'Vulnerable' by the IUCN. CITES list *C. niloticus* in both categories I and II, and ESA lists

**Nile crocodile**

it as 'Endangered'. Areas with healthy wild populations still permit limited harvesting, but in depleted areas there is a total ban and enforcement is reasonable. Breeds well in captivity and in reserves; thus, good potentiality for restocking depleted areas.

**Reproduction:**

A hole nester, that lays large clutches of eggs and protects nest site and young vigorously.

**Predator/Prey:**

A well-justified, notorious reputation as an agile, mean, fast man-killer. In certain areas adults eat and hunt a variety of mammals both small and large, for example buffalo, zebra and wildebeest as well as fish, birds and smaller crocodiles.

**African slender-snouted crocodile**

# African Slender-snouted Crocodile
## *Crocodylus cataphractes*

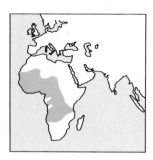

**Description:**

A dark-coloured, secretive, slender-snouted species with darker blotches on its jaws and stripes on its tail. Unlike that of other crocodiles, the neck armour is arranged in three rows, each composed of only two large scales that are joined to the back plates.

**Habitat and Distribution:**

Thought to be a freshwater species found in the tropical rainforests of West and Central Africa.

**Status:**

CITES I, ESA 'Endangered' and IUCN 'Indeterminate'. There is some hunting for hides and by local peoples for food.

**Reproduction:**

Builds mound nests along banks of streams and produces small clutches of eggs. Animals do not synchronize mating and egg-laying.

**Predator/Prey:**

Narrow snout indicates a fish-eating mode but is thought to take snails, crustaceans and frogs.

# Mugger Crocodile
## *Crocodylus palustris*

India, Sri Lanka, Pakistan, Nepal and eastward as far as southern Iran.

**Status:**

Listed in CITES II and as 'Vulnerable' by the IUCN; however, ESA lists this species as 'Endangered' due to heavy hunting for hides, habitat destruction and accidental entrapment in fishing gill nets. Also hunted for body parts for local healers who use them as

# New Guinea Crocodile
## *Crocodylus novaeguineae*

**Description:**

A narrow-snouted species with dark bands and spots, similar in appearance but somewhat larger, up to 4 m (13 ft), than the Philippine crocodile, *C. mindorensis*.

**Habitat and Distribution:**

Freshwater rivers, swamps and lakes of both coasts of New Guinea.

**Status:**

Despite being exploited under government management, it still exists in considerable numbers in the wild. Listed in CITES II; listed as 'Vulnerable' by IUCN. Captive breeding on private and government-sponsored farms.

**Reproduction:**

A mound nester with both parents caring for the nest. Southern population nests during wet season and northern population in the dry season.

**Predator/Prey:**

An opportunistic generalist.

**Mugger crocodile**

**Description:**

Also known as the marsh crocodile, these broad- and heavy-snouted crocodiles have the broadest heads of any of the Crocodylinae. Adults are uniformly grey-brown, while young are light brown with conspicuous darker bands. Adult males average about 4 m (13 ft), although some larger ones have been reported.

**Habitat and Distribution:**

These large animals dwell in marshes, rivers, swamps, ponds, lagoons, and man-made bodies of water, usually above salt water, but some populations also live in brackish waters. Found in

medicinals. Despite protective laws, poachers and egg-hunters extract a heavy toll. The Indian government is sponsoring a reintroduction programme of muggers bred in captivity.

**Reproduction:**

A hole nester; the only crocodilian known to lay two clutches of eggs per year. About 30 eggs per clutch.

**Predator/Prey:**

Despite reports of human remains in their stomachs and anecdotal reports of man-eating, this species is not considered a threat to humans. Large adults are known to take buffalo and deer as well as fish.

New Guinea crocodile

# Philippine Crocodile
## *Crocodylus mindorensis*

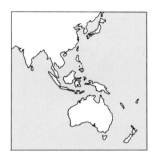

**Description:**

A relatively broad-nosed crocodile, 2.4–2.7 m (8–9 ft), with heavy neck and dorsal scales. Its colour is golden tan with dark blotches and dark stripes on the tail.

**Habitat and Distribution:**

Freshwater swamps, lakes and rivers. Found only in the Philippine Islands of Mindoro, Negros, Mindanao and Samar.

**Status:**

Heavily hunted for its hides and suffering from habitat destruction, only about 100 remain in the wild. Listed as 'Endangered' by IUCN and ESA and included in CITES I. Limited captive breeding.

**Reproduction:**

Not much known about this mound nester.

**Predator/Prey:**

Probably a generalist.

Philippine crocodile

## Siamese Crocodile
### *Crocodylus siamensis*

### Description:

Similar in appearance but smaller, about 3.7–4.0 m (12–13 ft), and broader-snouted than the Indopacific crocodile (*C. porosus*), with whom it shares its range. Tan with black stripes and many scales on its throat.

### Habitat and Distribution:

Found in freshwater swamps, rivers and lakes in South-east Asia: Thailand, Cambodia, Laos, Malay Peninsula and parts of Indonesia.

### Status:

Thought to be virtually extinct in the wild, mainly due to habitat destruction to create rice paddies. Listed as 'Endangered' by IUCN and ESA, and included in CITES I. Over 5,000 are commercially farmed at Samutpraken near Bangkok, although they are often hybridized with Indopacific crocodiles. Development of zoo breeding.

### Reproduction:

A mound nester, 20 to 50 eggs per clutch in captivity.

### Predator/Prey:

An opportunistic generalist.

**Siamese crocodile**

## Indopacific Crocodile
### *Crocodylus porosus*

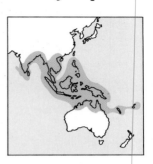

### Description:

A very large species, up to 7 m (23 ft) in length and weighing over 900 kg (2000 lb). Voracious, mean, handsome and widely distributed, this species is sometimes referred to as the 'saltwater crocodile' or 'estuarine crocodile' because it freely enters salt water and has been seen at sea hundreds of miles from land. Adults are tan to grey to black with a yellow or cream-coloured abdomen. Some light-coloured adults retain the dark stripes and blotches that are so conspicuous in the young. Their dorsal armour is composed of even, rounded scales. 'Salties' achieved a measure of fame as the villain in the film *Crocodile Dundee*. This crocodile has a well-documented history of man-eating, thus its notorious reputation is thoroughly deserved.

### Habitat and Distribution:

Usually found in freshwater rivers and lakes, although its tremendous capacity for osmoregulation (controlling internal levels of salt and water) means that it is often seen in saltwater estuaries and at sea. Because of its capacity for long-distance oceanic swimming, it resides on islands of the tropical Indopacific wherever suitable habitat presents itself, from eastern India and Sri Lanka, eastwards through South-east Asia, New Guinea and the Philippines, to coastal northern Australia and the Solomons. The easternmost limit of the Indopacific crocodile seems to be the Fiji Islands.

**Status:**

Extensively hunted for its hide. Because of habitat destruction some populations have been seriously depleted while others are well protected. Limited controlled harvesting from wild populations is permitted. Thus, the 'saltie' is listed in both CITES I and II while ESA and IUCN both list the species as 'Endangered'. Captive breeding and commercial farming provide animals to reintroduce into wild areas that have previously been depleted. Although protected, there is some resistance to reintroduction, given this animal's size, strength and aggressive disposition.

**Reproduction:**

Builds mound nests with up to 80 eggs. Parents guard nest; maternal care of hatchlings.

**Predator/Prey:**

Large adults eat anything they want to eat, from fish to large mammals, including humans, and are thought to be responsible for a number of supposed shark attacks.

Indopacific crocodile

## Australian Freshwater Crocodile
### *Crocodylus johnsoni*

### Description:

Also known as Johnston's crocodile, this medium-sized crocodilian averages 2.1 m (7 ft) in length, with rare individuals reaching 3 m (10 ft). A narrow-snouted species, it is brownish in colour with dark bands on the tail and body. Dorsal armour is six scales wide and the ventral scales are large.

### Habitat and Distribution:

A freshwater dweller found in lagoons, rivers and billabongs of northern Australia.

### Status:

Although its populations were seriously depleted by hide hunters, today it is well protected throughout its range and the indigenous populations seem to be recovering. Extensively farmed and ranched, it is listed in CITES II and as 'Vulnerable' by IUCN.

### Reproduction:

Digs hole nests during the dry season. Periodic droughts result in high egg and young mortality.

### Predator/Prey:

Feeds on fish, insects and other invertebrates, small amphibians, mammals and birds.

## African Dwarf Crocodile
### *Osteolaemus tetraspis*

### Description:

A very small, up to 1.8 m (6 ft), short-snouted, highly adaptable, forest-dwelling, nocturnal crocodile. Adults are brown-eyed, uniformly dark in colour, and have sturdy armoured skin on their necks and backs. Even their side ventral scales and tails are heavily armoured.

### Habitat and Distribution:

Found in slow-moving forest waters of West and Central Africa, often overlapping the range of the African slender-snouted crocodile, *C. cataphractus*.

### Status:

Although protected by law, enforcement is poor. While populations have been reduced, it is still abundant in many areas. It is on the CITES I list, while the IUCN lists it as 'Intermediate' and ESA as 'Endangered'. Although it breeds well in captivity, it is not farmed and no reintroduction programmes exist.

**Freshwater crocodile**

# American Alligator
## *Alligator mississippiensis*

American alligator

### Description:

Large, blackish-olive adult males larger than females. Juveniles have numerous yellow bands on tail and part of the body; hatchlings display bright yellow stripes in female. Snouts are long and equally broad for most of their length; the nostrils project. There is some variation of skull widths and shapes, with captive specimens having very broad skulls and rounded snouts. Some animals have bony plates in their ventral scales; others don't. Among the longest-lived crocodilians, they can grow to considerable sizes, 4.9–6.1 m (16–20 ft). However, due to extensive exploitation for meat and skin, few living specimens reach that size.

### Habitat and Distribution:

Primarily a freshwater inhabitant of still or slow-moving rivers, swamps, marshes and lakes. Some populations in coastal plains and lowlands can tolerate salt water for only brief periods since they lack salt glands. Populations reach as far north as the southern Virginia-North Carolina border, and extend southwards all the way to the Rio Grande in Texas.

### Status:

Recently removed from CITES I to CITES II and newly listed by IUCN as 'Out of danger'. Populations in some areas have experienced considerable growth and controlled hunting is now allowed in some states. Extensive ranching, farming and restocking efforts have been successful in increasing numbers. Population estimated at one million.

### Reproduction:

A mound nester, laying variable numbers of eggs. A 20-year-old female is capable of laying 60 or more eggs per clutch. Courtship starts late April, with mating in early May. Eggs laid mid-June, but each population varies with temperature. After about 65 days' incubation, nine to 10 hatchlings emerge. Mothers guard nest and protect hatchlings; strong maternal behaviour is exhibited by this species.

### Predator/Prey:

Adults immune to attack except by humans and other alligators. Eggs eaten by opossums, raccoons and black bears; hatchlings by ospreys, large fish, turtles and herons. Hatchlings feed on insects and crustaceans; the young feed on reptiles, small mammals and birds. Adults prefer small herbivores, also pet dogs. There are a few well-documented attacks on humans: 13 per year in Florida. Some deaths have been recorded.

African dwarf crocodile

## Chinese Alligator
### *Alligator sinensis*

**Chinese alligator**

**Description:**

A smaller version of the American alligator, *A. mississipiensis* (and possibly its ancestor). It averages about 1.8 m (6 ft), although maximal lengths of 3 m (10 ft) were reported some 3,000 years ago. Its head is large and its eyelids have bony plates. The snout narrows anteriorly and turns up slightly. Vertical scales have bony plates and no sensory pits.

**Habitat and Distribution:**

Restricted to marshes, ponds and lakes along the lower Yangtse basin in China. Digs dens and burrows.

**Status:**

Due to extensive habitat destruction, its natural range and population have been reduced. Today there are only about 500 specimens in the wild and in breeding facilities. Listed in CITES I and as 'Endangered' by both IUCN and ESA. Protected by the Chinese government. The Chinese alligator is being bred successfully for eventual restocking.

**Reproduction:**

A mound nester like the American alligator. Courts and mates in the spring and lays eggs in July. Hatchlings in late October.

**Predator/Prey:**

Adults of the species are passive and do not attack humans. Eats snails, freshwater clams, insects and small mammals.

## Common Cayman
### *Caiman crocodilus*

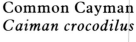

**Description:**

Also called the spectacled cayman because of a bony ridge running between the eyes like the bridge of a pair of spectacles. There are at least four similar subspecies, all of which have dark olive bodies and greenish irises. Their snouts taper giving them a crocodile-like look. Adult males average about 2.5 m (8 ft), with females of the same age being much smaller.

**Habitat and Distribution:**

Highly variable since this species is extremely adaptable. Small populations of former imported pets even manage to thrive in drainage canals of southern Florida, USA. Prefers open areas of lakes, swamps, rivers and cattle ponds. Despite heavy hunting, there is still an estimated population of more than 5 million. Found from southern Mexico and Central America to the Amazon and Orinoco basins, as far south as the temperate zone of northern Argentina.

**Status:**

Most are listed in CITES II, but one subspecies is included in CITES I. Two subspecies are listed as 'Endangered' by the ESA, and IUCN considers one species 'Vulnerable'.

**Common cayman**

# Broad-snouted Cayman
## *Caiman latirostris*

**Cuvier's dwarf cayman**

## Description:

A wide, heavily rounded, alligator-like head with dark blotches on the jaw. Overall colour is dark olive. Adult males reach a size of 3 m (10 ft), but female adults are much smaller, about 1.8 m (6 ft).

## Habitat and Distribution:

Found in shallow waters of swamps, mangrove forests, lakes and rivers of northern Argentina, south-east Brazil, Uruguay and Paraguay.

## Status:

Due to extensive habitat destruction caused by swamp drainage, highway and dam construction, urban developments and pollution, this species has suffered heavily. Listed in CITES I and as 'Endangered' by IUCN, it receives some governmental protection throughout its range, although such protection is generally poorly enforced. Its decline in population has been rapid throughout its range.

## Reproduction:

Mound nester; lays large clutches, up to 10 eggs.

## Predator/Prey:

This species eats snails, small mammals, fish, birds.

**Broad-snouted cayman**

# Cuvier's Dwarf Cayman
## *Paleosuchus palpebrosus*

## Description:

A very small crocodile whose maximal adult length is 1.5 m (5 ft) for males, 1.2 m (4 ft) for females. Its short snout and high, smooth skull are distinctive. It has small, dorsally projecting double tail scutes. Its belly has dark spots and the iris of its eye is chestnut-coloured.

## Habitat and Distribution:

Found in northern and central Amazon basin in flooded forests along the steep banks of streams and tributary entrances to lakes where the water flows rapidly. Prefers areas with stony beds.

## Status:

Because its tough, highly armoured skin is unsuitable for exploitation, this smallest of crocodiles is not uncommon. It is listed under CITES II and is considered not threatened by IUCN.

## Reproduction:

Not much is known about the habits of this species, except that it is a mound nester.

## Predator/Prey:

This species poses no threat to humans. It eats fish despite its short snout, also preying on a wide variety of invertebrate animals.

## Schneider's Dwarf Cayman
### *Paleosuchus brigonatus*

### Description:

Also called the smooth-snouted cayman or narrow-snouted cayman. This is a small, heavily-armoured, short-tailed, muscular species, measuring 1.4–1.7 m (4.5–5.5 ft). It and other members of its genus lack an armoured ridge between the eyes. They have large, sharp, triangular scutes on the dorsal surface and a broad, flat tail that is so heavily armoured it curtails the animal's movement. It seldom basks.

### Habitat and Distribution:

Found in small, high-banked, rapidly flowing, forested streams. Adults often hide from predators on land in fallen logs and burrow under forest debris. It is widespread in the Orinoco and Amazon River basins of tropical South America.

**Schneider's dwarf cayman**

### Status:

Because of its extraordinarily tough, heavily armoured skin, this species has not been exploited by hide hunters and is considered common throughout its range. It enjoys a CITES II listing and has an IUCN listing of 'Unthreatened'.

### Reproduction:

Builds mound nests prior to rainy season. Small clutches of eggs (about 10) hatch during the long rains.

### Predator/Prey:

Opportunistic feeders on both vertebrates and invertebrates. Larger forms show an affinity for pacas, a large rodent most commonly found along streams.

**Black cayman**

## Black Cayman
### *Melanosuchus niger*

### Description:

A very large cayman whose general appearance is similar to that of the American alligator, *Alligator mississippiensis*. Young have yellow-green and white spots and stripes on their grey-brown heads. Adults are blackish but retain the brownish-black blotched head. Male adults reach sizes of 6 m (20 ft) or more.

### Habitat and Distribution:

Slow-moving rivers, flooded edges of lakes and forests, sometimes on open beaches throughout much of the Amazon basin.

### Status:

Because of its habit of preying on cattle, the black cayman is hunted heavily by local populations. Not known as a man-eater, although there have probably been isolated incidents. Listed in CITES I and considered 'Endangered' by both IUCN and ESA. Despite being protected by laws, enforcement is poor.

### Reproduction:

Mound builder probably similar to the American alligator.

### Predator/Prey:

Adults eat fish, reptiles (including other species of cayman), and large mammals such as domestic cattle.

FOUR

REPRODUCTION AND
SOCIAL LIFE

## REPRODUCTIVE CYCLE

Temporal synchronization of female and male production of gametes (eggs and sperm) is absolutely necessary for all crocodilians. It appears that the annual mating cycle is mainly geared to temperature, although in some species the seasonal biological clock in their brains is set by the annual rainfall or water level in swamps and lakes. This is certainly true of the Indopacific crocodile (*Crocodylus porosus*) of the Northern Territory of Australia, where the overall reproductive strategy is both temperature- and rainfall-dependent.

*BELOW:* A young American alligator breaks out of its egg to enter a very hostile world.

Most seasonally reproductive animals depend on the brain's clock activating the master control centre in the hypothalamus. Releasing factors given off by the hypothalamus then activate the anterior pituitary, which in turn secretes gonadotrophic hormones. The two gonadotrophic hormones trigger gamete (eggs and sperm) production in both males and females and also stimulate the release of male and female sex hormones. These sex hormones not only prepare the reproductive organs for mating but are also responsible for the behaviours associated with reproduction, such as sex drive, courtship displays, nest building and maternal care. The hor-

mones in this case are not by themselves responsible for the behaviours but prime other centres in the brain that control them to respond to an array of sensory signals that are necessary to bring the whole process to fruition.

In temperate-dwelling crocodilians such as the American and Chinese alligators (*Alligator mississippiensis* and *A. sinensis*), the annual reproductive cycle is totally dependent on seasonal changes in temperature. During the cooler times of the year both males and females stop eating and spend most of their time in dens or holes, although they do emerge on warm, sunny days to bask in the sun. As the days grow warmer they depart their winter habitat, going into deeper water. At this time both sexes begin to bellow just prior to sunrise, and then resume their feeding activity. As the temperature increases, sexually mature adult animals begin a rather noisy and highly visual courtship behaviour, and the testes of mature adult males reach their greatest size, producing large numbers of viable sperm. Sperm production (spermatogenesis) begins earlier and lasts longer in the largest males.

The onset of spermatogenesis is in large part temperature-dependent. In one population of American alligators living in the Savannah River nuclear facility where the hot-water effluent from five nuclear reactors warmed the lake, the onset of sperm production was accelerated by a whole month. However, at the end of the breeding season the testes dramatically decrease in size and spermatogenesis ceases. Parallel changes in the female correspond in time to those of the male, thus synchronization of both egg and sperm production and of sexual appetite and receptivity occurs.

## SOCIAL BEHAVIOUR ASSOCIATED WITH REPRODUCTION

As early as the latter part of the sixteenth century there were reports of American alligators creating a chorus of resounding, thunderous roars and bellows during the breeding season. Recently, these vocal displays were studied in detail by K.A. Vliet of the University of Florida, and they revealed a more complex pattern of sounds and movements than are seen in any other living reptile. Sound communication is particularly valuable to the amphibious lifestyle since water is a better conductor of sound than air. These vocalizations occur with daily regularity during the breeding season. They usually start with one animal, and soon – within 30 seconds – others join in to produce a chorus of bellows. Sometimes bellowing can be triggered by environmental sounds such as the thunderous supersonic boom caused by aircraft, and experiments with a variety of musical instruments suggest that the note B-flat activates bellowing.

*ABOVE:* Early explorers of the southern United States reported hearing a thunderous chorus of bellows coming from alligator-infested swamps and lakes. Bellowing is sometimes done alone and sometimes in a chorus. Here, two alligators bellow together as a part of the courtship ritual.

There are a number of components associated with bellowing that follow a predictable sequence. The animal raises its head well out of the water and forcibly gulps in air to the point that the chest visibly inflates and its throat puffs. This is followed by a further raising of the head to about 40 degrees and an arching of the tail. The male then tenses his muscles to the point that the body vibrates and the water above the chest suddenly dances, giving the appearance of upside-down rainfall. These so-called subaudible vibrations, below 10 Hz, are thought to be conducted through the water for a considerable distance and are read by receptive females who home in on the sexually active male producing these sounds. To date 10 species of crocodilians have been observed to produce the water dance. Recent research has revealed that elephants and several other types of animals also communicate over considerable distances by means of subaudible sounds.

The subaudible vibrations are quickly followed by a deep, prolonged (about 6.5 seconds in duration) roar that is carried about 150 m (500 ft) over open marshland. The thunderous bellowing of the males is soon answered by other males and nearby females whose response is just a bit shorter and less vigorous than the males'. Bellowing occurs in bouts of five or six roars in the early morning or late afternoon, and the chorus may last for 10 minutes or more. Although experts are not certain of the function of bellowing, clearly it plays some role as a sexual attractant. The bellow may constitute an advertisement of size and strength and also may define territories, since large dominant animals with bigger voice-boxes produce deeper sounds. Males tend to fight more viciously

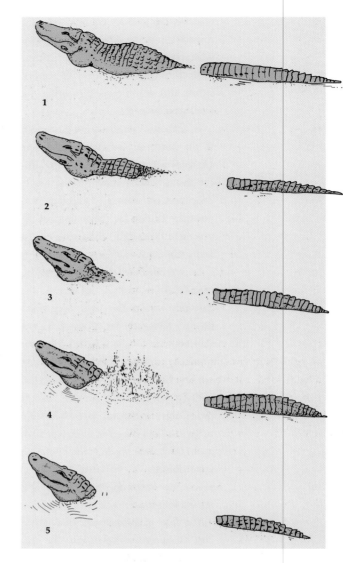

*RIGHT:* A sequence showing movements and postures displayed by male American alligators prior to bellowing. After the work of Dr Kent Vliet of the University of Florida.
*FROM TOP TO BOTTOM:*
(1) The alligator inhales deeply; (2) head is lowered; (3) head tilted and tail arched; (4) the animal generates subaudible vibrations and the water over its back dances; (5) a loud bellowing roar is emitted.

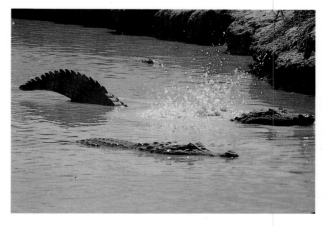

*RIGHT:* Sometimes during courtship, as the lovers swim side by side, both emit sub-audible vibrations. It may be presumed that these vibrations signal a measure of sexual excitement, but their exact function is not known at this time.

in the early courtship period when bellowing choruses are most frequent. Intention to attack by dominant males is signalled by another sound, a rumbling, low-intensity growl.

Bellowing is often accompanied by yet another acoustic signal, produced by slapping the head on to the water and loudly snapping the jaws shut. During this display the animals assume a motionless, elevated posture with much of the dorsal surface above the water. The crocodilian then begins to wag its arched tail vigorously. Some males at this point inflate themselves and generate subaudible vibrations, an exclusively male behaviour. The animals then open their jaws and smash the underside of their heads on to the water's surface while simultaneously clapping their jaws shut, thereby creating a loud sound that can be heard onshore more than 200 m (220 yd) away. In the water the sound undoubtedly travels much farther. Frequently during the courtship jawclap display the animals also growl. Both males and females produce this type of display, but males do it more frequently, and both sexes usually seek out specific sites to perform this type of behaviour. Males also tend to follow the headslap display by lunging forward towards another displayer. Like the bellowing, the headslap display seems to be contagious.

All crocodilians vocalize to some degree, but the American alligator, the Chinese alligator and the common cayman (*Caiman crocodilus*) are among the most vocal. As would be expected, there are some species differences in the characteristics of vocalization that are necessary in areas where two or more species co-exist.

*RIGHT:* A sequence of body postures and movements made by male American alligators during the head slap and jaw clap display described by Dr Kent Vliet.
*FROM TOP TO BOTTOM:*
(1) Head and body elevated; (2) head oblique with tail arched; (3) tail wags with head up; (4) jaws agape and subaudible vibrations; (5) head slap and jaws clap shut almost at the same time; (6) an inflated posture.

*RIGHT:* The head-slapping display shown here is an attention-getting display that is sometimes associated with courtship and sometimes associated with signalling dominance or territoriality.

## TERRITORIALITY AND DOMINANCE HIERARCHIES

In group-living animals such as crocodilians, many animals of different sexes, ages and sizes frequently aggregate and interact socially. Often the associations are loosely organized and the animals tend to ignore each other. At other times they are well organized, and large numbers of adults may be peacefully observed exploiting a food source such as a large dead mammal. Territoriality and dominance interactions, particularly between adult and subadult males, are a common feature of crocodilian behaviour, but such energy-consuming interactions are suspended during environmentally stressful times such as droughts.

Dominance is expressed by the strongest, largest, most aggressive members of the group to control access to space, food and females. The dominant male sends out an array of signals to ensure this control, especially when they form breeding groups during the courtship period. Dominant animals conspicuously display their size, and subdominant animals usually stay partially submerged and send out submissive signals. Sometimes, submissive small animals are attacked repeatedly, often losing bits and pieces of their tails or rear limbs and, in some cases, are actually killed by the dominant animals.

Combat between two heavyweight adults of equal size involves an orgy of heavy head blows. The Australian salties (*Crocodylus porosus*) are particularly violent as two males swim side by side, turning their rock-hard, bony heads away from each other and then, using their powerful neck muscles, simultaneously

smashing their heads together with such force that a loud thud can be heard. Such dominance battles may continue for more than an hour. In other species of large crocodilians, dominance battles involve biting and snapping each other's heads. Not much damage appears to be done during these encounters, and the end result is that one individual establishes himself as the dominant one. Social hierarchies based on size and strength are also seen in subadults and in females.

*BELOW:* Two American crocodiles head-bashing, a method of determining social hierarchies.

*FACING PAGE, BOTTOM:* As a part of their courting behaviour, females often have to repeatedly entice the apparently indifferent male. One of these behaviours includes the female climbing on the back of the reluctant object of her affection.

*RIGHT AND FACING PAGE, TOP:* Courtship by American alligators is initiated by the female nuzzling the snout and head of the male, which are richly endowed with sensory receptors. Such inciting behaviour evokes the male's response.

*BELOW:* Two American crocodiles are shown during their protracted courtship rituals. Both males and females will frequently mate with several different partners during the mating period.

## CROCODILIAN COURTSHIP

Courtship rituals in all animals entail a prolonged, often subtle collection of visual, tactile, olfactory and audible signals that are referred to as incitement behaviours. In crocodilians most courtship displays are initiated by the female, who first must turn off the innate aggressive programme of the male whose territory she has invaded. The female submissively lifts her head, exposing her vulnerable throat; this display signals peaceful intent. Initially, most males seem indifferent to the amorous advances of the female, but a persistent female will nuzzle the sides of the male's head and neck, erogenous zones which are richly endowed with touch receptors. Her repertoire of incitement behaviour then becomes a little bolder, and includes nudging, stroking and pushing, bumping him gently and even climbing on to his back and sliding over his head. All crocodilians have musk glands under their chins and in their cloacas that secrete a sweet-smelling, greenish, oily perfume which serves as a chemical message of sexual arousal.

Once the male gets the unambiguous message, he begins to respond and caresses back, touching, pushing, bumping, grunting, submerging and blowing bubbles. This period of sexual foreplay is quite protracted, but finally it is time for coupling. The male and female orient themselves side to side, the male presses down the female's head with his own, deftly lifts both of his legs on one side, then climbs on to her. The mating pair position themselves so that their cloacal openings are juxtaposed, he atop the female, she firmly embraced by his forelegs; he slides his body around hers until the bases of their tails are together. In a somewhat bizarre contortion their swollen cloacas make contact and the male organ enters the female. They remain in this coupled position in the water for several minutes and insemination occurs as the

*LEFT:* The courtship behaviours of crocodilians are many and varied. One frequently seen behaviour is bubble blowing. Here a male Indopacific crocodile courts his true love by submerging and blowing bubbles.

*BELOW LEFT:* Here the photographer is chest deep in the water photographing an American alligator climbing on to a consenting female just before insemination.

semen moves down a groove on the ventral side of the penis. The semen is then transported up the oviduct where fertilization occurs. Enough semen is transferred at this time to fertilize as many eggs as the female releases, which in some cases numbers more than 100. It is thought that the very process of copulation serves to trigger the release of eggs from the ovary.

The courtship period is lengthy – over a month long – and during this period the dominant member of a breeding group of males often mates with several different females. Depending on the species this number may vary from one to 20 females. The male's promiscuity is often matched by the female's who also mates with a number of subdominant males during the courtship period, although such activity is challenged by the dominant male.

# NESTING

All crocodilians lay their eggs on land in exposed sites, usually within 9 m (30 ft) of the water, in a specially prepared site or 'nest'. Two basic types of nests are prepared: hole nests and mound nests. The latter are raised structures composed of sand and earth combined with a great deal of plant material (grasses, water reeds and leaves), the decay of which releases heat to help insulate the eggs. The number of eggs laid in each nest varies from five to 150 eggs, depending on the species and the size and age of the female. The larger the female, the larger the size of the clutch of eggs, although every old females produce fewer eggs. The eggs are porcelain-white, hard-shelled and usually about the size of large chicken or duck egg (50–70 g). Usually, only one clutch of eggs is laid per year, although sometimes the mugger crocodile (*Crocodylus palustris*) produces two clutches per year. Some animals such as the hole-nesting Nile

*BELOW:* Crocodilians build either hole nests or mound nests. The mound nests contain a considerable amount of vegetation which generates heat as it decays. This heat aids in incubating the buried eggs. Here an American alligator sits astride her mound nest.

*ABOVE:* The number of eggs laid in a nest varies from species to species and also with the age of the mother. This picture shows an alligator nest that has been opened by a researcher. The eggs have hard white shells and are slightly larger than a jumbo-sized hen's egg.

crocodile *(C. niloticus)* utilize the same nesting ground year after year, and there is evidence that mound nesters such as the American alligator use the same nest site repeatedly. A typical mound nest is about 1.5–2.1 m (5–7 ft) in diameter and is 0.5–1.0 m (1.5–3.0 ft) high. These nests are usually near an excavated well or den that the female uses as a refuge during nesting or as a site for overwintering.

Nest-building precedes egg-laying by several weeks, with some hole-digging species actually digging test or trial holes to ascertain optimal incubating conditions. The hole is excavated with the hind feet, and the excavated soil is subsequently

used to cover the eggs. Sometimes the female lays part of the clutch, covers those eggs with sand and then lays the rest of the eggs on top of the first layer. It is thought that hole-nesting is evolutionarily more primitive than mound-nesting. Mound-nesting species first gather a collection of leaves, grasses, reeds and other plant litter at the selected nesting site and then create a mound using this plant material combined with earth or sand. The mother then compacts all the material into a firm, solid mound. Finally she excavates a cavity up to 60 cm (2 ft) deep, lays her eggs and covers them up.

A number of environmental factors such as flooding, droughts and abnormally high or low temperatures can affect embryo mortality in the nest. Although several crocodilian species are known to protect their nests from intruders, several species of predators have specialized in raiding nest sites. American alligators' mound nests are often exposed by raccoons, opossums and black bears, while the hole nests of Nile crocodiles are frequently plundered by monitor lizards, baboons and hyenas. In South America, cayman nests are reportedly most often attacked by tegu lizards and ring-tailed coatis.

Nesting in dense tropical rainforest where there is little direct sunlight filtering through the canopy poses a problem for Schneider's dwarf cayman (*Paleosuchus brigonatus*) of the Amazon and Orinoco basins. How does it keep the nest warm enough to incubate the eggs? Being a mound-nester, some heat is generated by the decay of the vegetable matter used to make the nest, and the metabolism of the developing embryo also contributes to overall heat production. But in case this is insufficient, Schneider's dwarf cayman uses yet a third thermal strategy that employs the metabolic heat generated by subterranean termites. To achieve this end the cayman builds its nest around a raised termite mound and places the egg chamber close to the mound where the temperature is relatively constant at 32°C (90°F). In this case the cayman has literally recruited the termites into a cooperative venture.

Another example of involuntary nesting cooperation is seen in the behaviour

of a snake, a lizard and three species of aquatic turtle whose reproductive cycle coincides with that of the American alligator. These animals exploit the raised mound nests made by the alligator to deposit their own eggs. The nest, being soft, easily warmed soil, is ideal for laying eggs. The nest is often also protected from egg-eating predators by the fiercely protective mother alligator; thus, the alligator is unwittingly also protecting the eggs of these other species.

## INCUBATION AND TEMPERATURE-DEPENDENT SEX DETERMINATION

In most animals sex determination is generally established at the time of fertilization; thus, in mammals, those having two X chromosomes will be female and those having one X and one Y chromosome will be male. In crocodilians sex is determined by incubation temperature. This has been experimentally proven in five species of crocodiles and three species of alligators and caymans, and is most probably true for all species. The duration of the incubation period is also temperature-dependent; thus, at 28°C (82°F) incuba-tion may last 100 days, while at 33°C (91°F) it may last only 70 days.

Sex is determined during the first few weeks of the incubation. If the tempera-tures are low (28–31°C/82–88°F), the off-spring are exclusively female, and femaleness is irreversibly set by 30 days. When the early incubation is kept at 33°C (91°F) or more the hatching will be exclusively male, and this is determined by the 45th day. If the temperature is maintained at an optimal temperature (31.5–32.5°C/89–90.5°F), there will be equal numbers of male and female hatch-lings. Excessively high incubation temperatures (above 34°C/93°F) and excessively low incubation temperatures

*ABOVE:* A mugger crocodile hatches. Muggers are the only crocodilians known to lay two clutches of eggs per year.

(below 27°C/81°F) are lethal for the developing embryo. The fact that natural populations in the wild produce approximately equal numbers of both genders is testimony to the engineering skill of crocodilian nest-building because, despite changes in environmental temperatures, the well-insulated, buried brood chamber maintains a constant temperature within narrow limits.

Temperature not only affects crocodilian overall reproductive strategy and sex determination but also affects pigmentation pattern of the hatchlings, hatchling size and post-hatchling growth rate and ability to regulate temperature.

FACING PAGE, ABOVE:
A young mugger
crocodile in the
process of hatching.
Some hatchlings
break the shell with
a projecting tooth.

FACING PAGE, BELOW:
Several species of
crocodilians may
help the hatchlings
to the water by
picking them up in
their mouths and
carrying them there.
Sometimes they also
pick up unhatched
eggs and exert a
gentle pressure to
crack the eggs open,
thereby speeding up
the hatching
process.

## HATCHING AND MATERNAL CARE

Young crocodilians prior to hatching begin to vocalize. Some think these audible messages play a role in synchronizing hatching time, and, indeed, there is remarkable temporal synchronization of hatching time. There is, however, no ambiguity about the role of prehatching vocalization (grunts) which acts as a signal to the nearby mother. On hearing their calls, she emerges from the water and begins to tear open the nest hole with her front feet and jaws. Some hatchlings punch a hole in the hard shell with a front projecting tooth; others may require help getting hatched. Often female crocodiles and alligators pick up unhatched, vocalizing eggs and roll them against the roof of their mouths to crack the egg shell and

liberate the young. The same jaws that, during a snap, can generate a pressure of a few thousand pounds per square inch, can be remarkably gentle. The released hatchlings then either follow their mother to nearby water or are carried to the water in her mouth.

The vocalizings of yelping, newly hatched Nile crocodiles evoke a similar response. The nearby mother excavates the nest chamber, picks up both hatchlings and unhatched eggs in her mouth, where their weight pushes down her tongue to form a pouch, and transports the hatchlings to the water. She also manipulates unhatched eggs to facilitate the release of the hatchlings. Similar responses have been observed in the mugger crocodile (*Crocodylus palustris*), except that both father and mother contribute to

BELOW: A mother
New Guinea
crocodile picking up
her newly hatched
young to carry them
to the water. Often
nearby predators
will dash in to
snatch eggs or
hatchlings while the
mother is
transporting some of
the young.

*LEFT:* A female New Guinea crocodile carrying eggs in her mouth. Despite the power of her jaw, she can exercise extremely delicate pressures and, by rolling the eggs across her tongue, can crack the eggs to help the hatchlings emerge. While in the egg, the hatchling emits sounds which tell the mother that hatching is imminent.

*RIGHT:* Young alligators, like their parents, are cold-blooded and regulate their body temperature by a variety of behaviours. Here, a brightly coloured American alligator basks in the sun.

next excavation, cracking the eggs and carrying the hatchlings to water, although sometimes the larger male claims the privilege for himself. The long-snouted, sharp-toothed gharyals (*Gavialis gangeticus*) do aid in freeing the hatchlings but neither crack eggs in their mouths nor carry the hatchlings to water.

The maternal devotion to duty during the lengthy incubation period, the hatching, and for several months to a year after hatching, is exceptional. The mother not only protects the nests (although predators may get 50% of the eggs), but guards the hatching with great vigour. When hatchlings are threatened, they give an alarm call that not only brings the concerned mother charging to their defence, but also often summons other nearby adults, both male and female, to drive away intruders.

Despite the defensive measures of the adults, many hatchlings fall prey to predators. Alligator hatchlings are devoured by large birds such as the blue-grey heron, and raptors such as the osprey. Other predators include large turtles, snakes and large catfish. Nile crocodile hatchlings are relentlessly hunted by African fish eagles and by a number of very large wading avian hunters such as the 2-m (6.5-ft)-tall Goliath heron. They are also hunted by jackals, hyenas, large mongooses and leopards as well as by predatory fish such as the ferocious 50-kg (110-lb) tiger fish and cat fish. Estuarine-dwelling hatchlings and juveniles may be preyed upon by sharks. Finally, many young fall victim to larger and older members of their own species: cannibalism among crocodilians is well documented.

It is true that there is safety in numbers, and hatchlings remain in the vicinity of

*LEFT:* Up to 50% of eggs are destroyed by nest raiders, while a majority of the hatchlings are picked off by a variety of predators like this large heron. Probably only two or three out of every hundred eggs develop into adults.

*ABOVE:* A hatching New Guinea crocodile starts to break through its shell.

*BELOW:* A Siamese crocodile emerges from its egg. Its exit from the egg is facilitated by a forward pointing hatching tooth.

their nests and congregate in large groups called 'creches', often under the protection of a nearby parent. This kind of communal aggregation is particularly noticeable in the American alligator, where several generations remain in a given territory. Often the female guardian will intimidate or attack intrusive larger juveniles and subadults who stray into their nursery areas.

As they grow older most crocodilians become less sociable, but individuals of about the same size do congregate in basking groups without fighting. In the event of a drought, animals of all sizes and ages assemble in large groups and, under such stress, seldom behave aggressively.

In captive breeding facilities, individual crocodilians often gather to form dense congregations, but captivity seems to dampen aggressiveness amongst these animals, and threat and attack in such conditions are relatively rare.

*BELOW:* Young alligators frequently gather together for mutual protection. Here a crèche of alligator hatchlings congregate.

# HUNTING AND
# FEEDING

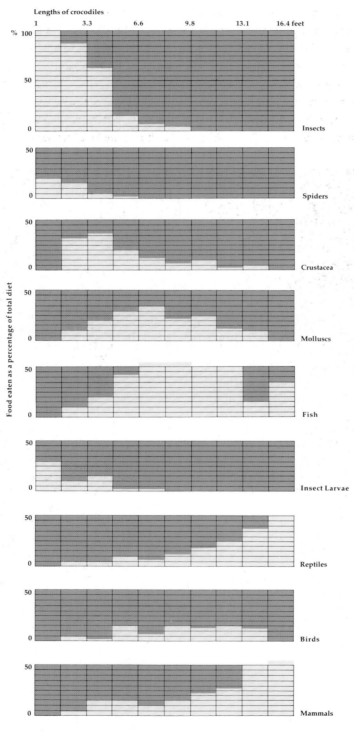

Lengths of crocodiles

1    3.3    6.6    9.8    13.1    16.4 feet

Food eaten as a percentage of total diet

Insects

Spiders

Crustacea

Molluscs

Fish

Insect Larvae

Reptiles

Birds

Mammals

Crocodiles, alligators and gharyals (gharials) are all superb, cold-blooded hunters, marvellously adapted to the role of stalking, capturing, killing and eating a variety of prey. The long-nosed species, the gharyal (*Gavialis gangeticus*), thought to be similar to ancient ancestral forms, the false gharyal (*Tomistoma schlegelii*) and some of the thin-snouted crocodiles, are primarily fish-eaters that capture their prey by means of a rapid sideways snap of their tooth-lined jaws. The advantage of the long, thin snout is that, during the quick, horizontal hunting snap, it can move through the water with much greater ease than can a broad snout.

The broad-nosed species are also fish-eaters, but their diets vary widely with species, age and availability of prey. As can be seen in the table at left young Nile crocodiles (*Crocodylus niloticus*), during their first years of life, subsist on a diet of insects, spiders, crabs, small frogs, snails and even aquatic insect larvae. They round up their prey by curving their bodies and snapping them up with a visually aimed sideways movement of the jaws. As broad-snouted crocodiles, caymans and alligators grow, their diet changes, and they begin to eat small mammals, aquatic birds, turtles and other reptiles, including other smaller members of their own species. Indeed, whenever one observes Nile crocodiles basking on the sandbars and river banks, one is struck by the fact that in any grouping all individuals are about the same size. At one place they are in the 3–3.5 m (10–12 ft) range, and at another site they are in the 1.5–1.8 m (5–6 ft) range. This behaviour is thought to be a self-preservation tactic that prevents the hungry, large crocodiles from cannibalizing their smaller cousins.

Most stalking and hunting occurs in the water and at the water's edge. The initial approach is slow and stealthy, the crocodile being almost totally submerged, with only its eyes, ears and nostrils showing above the surface. It propels itself forward by undulating its oar-like tail, and while swimming it assumes a streamlined configuration by holding its fore- and hindlimbs closely against its body.

The approach is so slow that barely a ripple is detectable, and as the hunter gets within range, it submerges completely until within 4.5–6.0 m (15–20 ft) of its prey. The actual attack is a sudden, rapid strike propelled by a few strokes of its powerful, muscular tail. The vice-like, tooth-lined jaws snap shut with enormous force of more than 200 kg/cm$^2$ (3,000 lb/sq in). Small prey are killed instantly

and swallowed whole, but large prey are grabbed and pulled into the water. Many of these prey are too large to swallow, hence after they have been drowned, their carcasses are gruesomely dismembered into bite-size portions. To achieve this the crocodilian grabs a chunk of its victim and then spins rapidly on its axis, twisting off large pieces of flesh, which are then swallowed. Since the conical, pointed teeth of crocodilians are not suitable for chewing or shredding, they swallow the whole mouthful they have twisted off. Because the crocodilian's tongue is fused to its lower jaw and is capable of very little movement, swallowing by lifting the tongue is impossible. Crocodilians take their mouthful, raise their heads to the surface and then literally throw the food down their throats with a series of jerky head movements. After swallowing, they take a few deep breaths and submerge for another mouthful.

Crocodilians with full stomachs (the stomach is about the size of a basketball) can also store food in the elastic oesophagus. For many years it was thought that digestion of ingested protein was aided by the stones found in their stomachs. Certainly, a number of birds have adopted this digestive strategy, but today that belief has been discarded. According to H. B. Cott (1961), the stones in the stomach function as ballast for these submersible hunters. The weight of stones in the stomach varies with the size of the crocodile, and a 500-kg (1,000-lb) specimen is likely to have about 5 kg (11 lb) of stones in its stomach.

Apparently, digestion is fairly rapid. Some indigestible material is regurgitated and spat out, while the remnants of the digestive process, the stool, are evacuated

from the rectum into the cloaca, from where they are vented into the water.

Although most attacks are launched at the water's edge, crocodiles and black caymans (*Melanosuchus niger*), despite their short legs, can move on land at considerable speed, albeit for only short distances. Sometimes on land they use their powerful, muscular tails or their bony, rock-hard heads as flails to knock their prey down. Such blows are strong enough to knock down most large mammals. On land the usual strategy is to drive the prey

*ABOVE:* A mugger crocodile enjoys a quick snack. Crocodiles' prey varies in size: nothing is too small and when minnows are abundant, crocodiles eat them by the dozen.

*BELOW:* Like all crocodilians, the Orinoco crocodile has a varied diet, eating any animal it can catch. Here a large South American rattlesnake is about to be ingested.

into the water, where the reptile enjoys a significant tactical advantage.

It is thought that hunting by crocodilians is primarily a visual process and that the slit-like eyes are heavily rod-dependent. This type of vision allows the hunter to distinguish black-and-white shapes of prey more than 9 m (30 ft) away in dim light and to detect quick movement at distances of 30 m (100 ft) or more. Crocodilians are also able to distinguish colours.

Crocodiles and alligators are opportunistic feeders and often eat carrion. There have even been reports of crocodiles lodging their prey under submerged roots or logs to let the tough flesh rot. The decaying flesh of a rotting carcass is much easier to tear off than the stringy flesh of a freshly killed animal. However, some experts disagree with this interpretation, based on the observation that well-fed crocodiles in captivity will eat only fresh wildebeest and others – are frequently

*LEFT:* Every year the wildebeest of the Serengeti Plains in Tanzania migrate. When they reach a water obstacle they charge in and there, waiting for them, are adult Nile crocodiles.

*RIGHT:* Another favourite food of adult Nile crocodiles is the zebra. Although always alert for predators, zebras are frequently surprised and fall victim to crocodiles.

*LEFT:* A common cayman scavenges a dead mullet from the shore.

HUNTING
AND
FEEDING

85

killed by flash floods, providing a free meal. A good-sized buffalo, weighing 680–900 kg (1,500–2,000 lb), will satisfy a number of crocodiles, which have been observed feeding cooperatively without fighting each other. Grimzek, in his chapter on crocodiles and alligators in *Encyclopedia of Animals*, reports them gathering in large numbers around a dead buffalo and, along with other scavengers, sharing the copious repast. Another frequent source of carrion are bull hippopotamuses which have been killed in fights with each other. According to Grimzek, the crocodiles can detect the carcass as far as 3 km (2 miles) distant (either by taste or by smell) and are quick to accept the olfactory invitation. In another report, 120 large crocodiles of more than 2 m (7 ft) congregated to feed cooperatively on a dead male hippopotamus.

## PREDATORS OF CROCODILIANS

As is the case with most egg-laying species, the greatest predation occurs upon eggs and young animals despite protective efforts by the mother. The Nile crocodile has very strong maternal instincts, and she carefully guards her nest, often sitting on top of it. Even when the sun's heat becomes too intense, she only withdraws to nearby shade or water where she can still stand guard. Nevertheless, a number of egg-eating species of birds, reptiles and mammals routinely raid the nest. The African monitor lizard is among the most voracious of egg-eaters. One monitor was seen to burrow under the nest while the mother crocodile sat on top of it, and another report describes an instance where a male monitor lured the defending mother crocodile from her nest to give his

mate a chance to descend upon the vacated clutch of eggs. A number of mammals also raid nests, particularly hyenas and mongooses. Several species of large predatory birds that are sometimes preyed upon by large crocodiles will 'gain revenge' by attacking an unprotected nest. Among the frequent avian raiders of nests are maribou storks.

The American alligator (*Alligator mississippiensis*), which builds raised-mound nests, exercises some guardianship of the nest site, but she is not so diligent a defender as her cousins, the Nile crocodile, the Indopacific crocodile (*Crocodylus porosus*) and the mugger crocodile (*C. palustris*). The main predators of alligator nests are the ubiquitous, black-masked raccoons and black bears.

*ABOVE:* All mammals come to the water to drink; Nile crocodiles observe their habits and stalk animals like this waterbuck at the shore's edge.

*FACING PAGE, ABOVE:* When young, most crocodilians rely on a diet that includes small lizards, insects and crustacea.

*RIGHT:* Large crocodiles will feed on large wading birds such as this 1.8 m (6 ft) tall goliath heron. More frequently, however, the goliath heron feeds on young crocodiles, particularly hatchlings which are swallowed whole.

*LEFT:* In the Florida Everglades up to 50% of the alligator eggs are destroyed by the ubiquitous black-masked raccoon. In areas of high predation, park rangers trap raccoons and move them to other areas.

BELOW: The principle airborne killer of young American alligators is the voracious osprey. When the insecticide DDT was in heavy use, the osprey population dropped dramatically because DDT caused the eggshells to weaken and break.

RIGHT: Large predatory birds like these fish eagles are among the major predators of first-year Nile crocodile hatchlings. Hawks and eagle owls also contribute to the devastating losses among hatchling crocodiles.

Once the young are hatched, the 18–23-cm (7–9-in) long hatchlings make their way to shallow water on their own or are carried there in the mother's mouth. Even though they are still protected by the mother, the next two years of life will see their numbers decrease rapidly as a variety of predators stalk and kill these vulnerable little reptiles. Some of the predators are other reptiles such as the monitor lizard that stalks the water's edge. In the water soft-shelled turtles and larger crocodiles will also take their toll despite the convoying efforts of the mother. Many young crocodiles are hunted by large predatory birds. In Africa the main avian threat is from the sharp-eyed fish eagle whose extraordinary eyesight permits it to see its target eight times larger and with more clarity than a human eye focusing over the same distance. In areas of dense fish eagle populations the young Nile crocodiles shift to a nocturnal behavioural pattern but in so doing become prey for the large, night-hunting owls and eagle owls. The American alligator's young are also hunted by large birds, primarily the osprey. In the water their enemies include large-mouthed channel catfish and large snapping turtles.

As the young reptiles grow to the point where they are no longer protected by their mothers, they adopt a furtive life-style and are seldom seen, hiding in weedy inlets, under bushes growing by the water, and in burrows that they dig out of the bank with their mouths. These burrows are located at approximately water level and provide protection from predators as well as warmth in the cool season and shade in the hot season. These burrows or tunnels often terminate in a large hollow cavity in which many juveniles of roughly the same size (60–90 cm/24–30 in) congregate, often peacefully stacked one upon another. The burrows are dug out cooperatively by several juveniles, providing refuge during the hot season when airborne hunters abound. In the final analysis the odds of a young crocodilian making it to the relatively invincible status of a full-grown adult are very low indeed. Estimates of achieving adult status range from 2% to less than 5%.

## PREDATORS OF ADULT CROCODILES

Even though they have been described as relatively invulnerable, adult crocodiles can fall foul of some large mammals. On occasion big cats coming to the water's edge to drink will be attacked by large crocodiles, and sometimes in such contests the crocodile loses. Lions have been seen to kill crocodiles in Africa, and in South America caymens have fallen victim to jaguars. Hippopotamuses share the African waters with crocodiles. These are awesomely powerful animals equipped with long, sharp tusks in their huge jaws. Hippopotamuses, particularly the males, have a very aggressive nature, and in Kenya they kill more people than do crocodiles. Their aggression increases during the mating season when bull hippopotamuses attack each other and often crocodiles and other animals too who happen to be in their territorial waters. Thus, it is not surprising that hippopotamuses, given their size, equipment and disposition, are one of the major killers of adult African crocodiles. An ancient Egyptian depiction of a hippopotamus with a large Nile crocodile in its jaws attests to this fact.

African elephants are also known to kill adult crocodiles. A female adult elephant may weigh up to 6 tonnes (5.9 tons) and is very protective of her young. As the sun rises elephants come to the rivers to bathe and drink. Sometimes a hungry adult crocodile will be driven to make a poor risk-benefit decision and attack a baby elephant. The crocodile is no match for the mother and is not only crushed to death but may even have its carcass hung on a tree by the river's edge. The reason for such elephant behaviour is obscure. Young caymans are also sometimes killed by large constrictor snakes such as the anaconda. But despite these infrequent events, the large, adult crocodilian is for the most part safe from all predators except humans.

## CROCODILE/BIRD SYNERGISM

Although birds make up a considerable portion of the crocodilian diet, there are some birds which crocodiles do not attack. This is because they have a synergistic relationship with these birds, i.e. both bird and crocodile benefit from the relationship. The first written report of such an interaction is attributed to the Greek historian and naturalist Herodotus, who described a shore bird picking leeches and other parasites off the skins and out of the gaping mouths of basking Nile crocodiles. Other stories by ancients – Aristotle, Aelianus and Pliny – recount similar bird behaviours, including teeth-

*BELOW:*

Hippopotamuses and crocodiles share the same habitat, often indifferent to each other's presence. Often the male hippos fight and kill each other during mating season and the loser's carcass is scavenged by crocodiles. Sometimes hippos will also attack a crocodile and their awesome armament of tusks can kill even adult crocodiles.

*FACING PAGE, ABOVE:*

Sometimes lions coming to drink are attacked by large Nile crocodiles. In such confrontations, either animal may triumph. Lions and other large cats such as the leopard are also known to prey on young sub-adult crocodiles caught on land.

cleaning and the emission of alarm calls to warn the crocodiles of approaching danger. This latter kind of behaviour has been observed in modern times. Spur-winged plovers that are often found in the company of crocodiles emit a shrill alarm cry when danger threatens, whereupon the crocodiles basking along the bank quickly slip into the water. This plover and other birds, such as the common sandpiper, have been seen walking around, on and even in the mouths of crocodiles. However, only one bird enjoys the distinction of having the common name of 'crocodile bird'. This is the Egyptian plover, a handsome bird with pale grey plumage on its back and pale yellow-white undersides. It has distinctive black stripes encircling its breast, from its beak to its eyes and on its cap, and is found throughout tropical climes, often around or on Nile crocodiles.

*LEFT:* Crocodiles judge potential prey by size. They never attack adult elephants, but small baby elephants are sometimes taken. These attacks usually bring the mother charging to the rescue and often results in a dead crocodile. There have been reports of elephants hanging dead crocodiles on trees, as if to post a warning.

## MAN-EATERS: FACT AND FICTION

Since the dawn of recorded history, crocodile attacks on humans living along the shores of lakes, rivers and estuaries have been described. Certainly, the larger crocodiles are capable of capturing and killing mammals much larger than human beings. Indeed, analyses of the stomach contents of Nile crocodiles in Uganda show that as they increase in size the relative proportion of mammals in their diet increases (see the table on page 82).

Some of the attacks on humans are simply a manifestation of crocodilian territoriality, and it is well documented that during the breeding season both males and females will fiercely protect their basking and nesting sites. The males are particularly pugnacious at these times, and there are a number of accounts of bull Nile crocodiles making unprovoked attacks on boats. Alistair Graham and Peter Beard in their fascinating, if somewhat bizarre, book *Eyelids of Morning: The Mingled Destinies of Crocodiles and Men* (New York Graphic Society, NY 1973) reported that the 5,500 adult Nile crocodiles of Lake Rudolf in Kenya '. . . are in the habit of dining regularly on Turkana children, women and elders.'

The bulk of reports of crocodile attacks on humans are attributed to the Nile crocodile and the Indopacific or estuarine crocodile, both of which are Old World species. These widespread species are found in suitable habitats throughout tropical Africa and on offshore islands,

*ABOVE:* Humans are sometimes victims of maneating crocodilians such as the Nile crocodile and the infamous saltwater crocodile of the Indopacific. This man is lucky to be alive after a brutal attack.

such as the Malagasy Republic (Madagascar), as well as tropical Asia. Their numbers have decreased in recent years with the increased availability of high-powered rifles, but prior to this these large predators must have been responsible for a great many human deaths.

Another crocodile that enjoys a sinister but possibly undeserved reputation as a man-eater is the Indian mugger crocodile (*C. palustris*), found in freshwater rivers of India and Sri Lanka. Rudyard Kipling in *The Undertakers* contributed to the mugger's dubious reputation:

'. . . Is there a green branch and an iron ring hanging over a doorway? The Old Mugger knows that a boy has been born in that house, and must some day come down to the Ghaut to play. Is a maiden married? The Old Mugger knows, for he sees the men carry gifts back and forth; and she, too, comes down to the Ghaut to bathe before her wedding, and – he is there.'

While there are some relatively recent reports of muggers attacking humans, the basis of their bad reputation comes from the finding of human remains and jewellery in their digestive tracts; but these remains are frequently charred and probably represent corpses from burning ghats along Indian and Sri Lankan rivers. The jewellery also may not indicate killing but merely items swallowed to provide ballast.

The two principal villains, the Nile and Indopacific crocodiles, are known to become more aggressive as they increase in size. Both have been known to stalk and attack humans. On the other hand, other very large crocodiles, such as the Orinoco

crocodile (*Crocodylus intermedius*) and the African slender-snouted crocodile (*C. cataphractus*), have no recorded history of attacks on humans. The relative aggression of the Nile crocodile seems to vary from place to place. I have observed children wading across the Samburu River in Kenya only 150 m (500 ft) from the Samburu Lodge where, for the entertainment of tourists, the staff feed crocodiles of some 3–4 m (10–13 ft) every evening.

This differential in aggressive behaviour is well documented. In some areas the local human population bathe and wash with relative impunity, while in other localities the inhabitants have built fences and stockades in the water to pro-

tect people filling water jugs and making their ablutions. Why such disparity exists may reflect the availability of other types of food.

As is the case with most examples of crocodilian predation on large animals, the attacks on humans are launched from the water. Once the victim has been seized in its powerful jaws, that person is pulled down under the water until he or she drowns, after which the victim is dismembered and eaten. Nobody knows for

*BELOW:* In some areas Nile crocodiles are known to be maneaters, while in other areas humans are seldom attacked. Shown here are two Samburu children making haste to cross the muddy river in Kenya's Buffalo Springs Park. Less than 914 m (1,000 yd) away, adult crocodiles come to the safari lodge every evening to be fed.

sure how often this scenario is repeated. In 1953 L. Earl estimated that as many as 1,000 people a year were killed by crocodiles on the lower Zambesi River alone. Another report claimed that a Nile crocodile measuring 4.6 m (15 ft 3 in) was responsible for over 300 deaths in its lifetime. Others feel that the hazard is grossly exaggerated and that the number of crocodile attacks on humans is almost nil. Given the mass slaughter of crocodilians all over the world, it is less likely that you will be killed by a crocodile than that you will be killed by a falling meteorite – that is, unless you live in Australia's Northern Territory.

The black caymans of the Amazon basin are noted for their pugnacity and are considered more vicious and likely to bite than any alligator or crocodile. There are numerous anecdotal accounts of attacks by black caymans but no authoritative reports of deliberate attacks on humans.

The recent film *Crocodile Dundee* brought home to cinema audiences worldwide the terror of the Indopacific crocodile of the northern provinces of Australia. Indeed, in 1979 Queen Elizabeth awarded a 13-year-old girl a medal for heroism for rescuing a full-grown man who had been attacked by a large crocodile. These big 'salties' frightened and attacked the earliest explorers and pioneers in northern Australia, as is dramatically shown in the painting by Thomas Baines of two of Sir Augustus Gregory's men killing a saltie during his 1855 expedition into the Northern Territory. It was a similar belligerent, 3-m (10-ft) saltie that attacked Captain Philip Darlington of the US Army in New Guinea in World War II. He was dragged underwater and twisted

about but fortunately was able to free himself and report the event.

Although in the latter part of the twentieth century the huge, sea-going Indopacific crocodiles were at one point considered an endangered species, they are now enjoying a comeback thanks to laws that have been enacted to protect them. They still pose a threat to humans in northern Australia. In 1980 there were four saltie attacks, two of them fatal, and in 1986–7 salties killed six more people. The conservationists trying to preserve these crocodiles found themselves caught in the middle: how could they manage a 6.4-m (21-ft), one-tonne potential man-eater while keeping an enraged, frightened public from taking matters into their own hands? The problem was similar to the ones faced by the US Park Service with man-killing grizzly bears and the Indian Park Service coping with man-eating tigers.

As is usually the case, pragmatism came to the fore. To prevent attacks and yet still conserve these magnificent reptiles, a public education programme was launched, crocodile ranching was encouraged and signs were erected:

'Beware. This is Crocodile Country. Swimming, fishing, gutting fish on a boat ramp and camping at waterholes is dangerous.'

Part of the problem is that the attempt to protect the saltie has been almost too successful. It is estimated that more than 50,000 of these crocodiles live in the Northern Territory today. This increase in numbers is matched by the growth of the human population in the area (over 140,000) and the influx of visitors seeking outdoor recreation. These two factors clearly increase the chances of human/ crocodile confrontation. Eric Hoffman in his article *Man Eater* describes a number of the more recent attacks in some detail. Because of these attacks, many salties have been killed by local citizens, and the Queensland government have begun a programme to remove salties over 1.8 m (6 ft) in length, to create saltie-free zones, and to exterminate known 'problem crocs'. Although the saltie still remains an unloved beast, the public attitude towards them, thanks to educational programmes, is much improved.

The American crocodile (*Crocodylus acutus*) of the mangrove estuaries in southernmost Florida grows to a length of 6 m (20 ft). An animal of this size certainly conjures up a feeling of unease. However, this large carnivore is simply not interested in people. There are two stories dating back to about 1900 of a hunter fatally injured by a wounded American crocodile; and A. W. Dimock in *Florida Enchantments* relates how a badly wounded crocodile bit a chunk out of his skiff. Other than these stories, the 500 or so American crocodiles in southern Florida have never once been reported over the last 70 years to threaten humans.

The American alligator (*Alligator mississippiensis*) enjoys a less benign reputation, although the number of recorded attacks on humans is still comparatively small. It has been estimated that less than 1% of human/American alligator confrontations result in an attack. There have also been reports of human remains and jewellery being found in the stomachs of dead alligators, but given the alligator's propensity for scavenging, the remains were probably those of drowned people.

What not to do

*LEFT:* Over the past several years, a number of people have been attacked and killed by the very aggressive saltwater crocodile. In Australia's Northern Territory, where many of these attacks occur, a major educational effort is under way to educate and warn the ever increasing numbers of tourists of the danger. Despite these warning signs, some people are still eaten.

Prior to 1977 there was no official documentation of alligator attacks on humans, although before that time sensationalist headlines in Florida newspapers luridly described the few attacks that did occur: 'The Jaws of Death Struck in Silence'; 'That Could Have Been My Child', etc. From the late 1960s up until today both alligator and human populations have grown significantly, and the juxtaposition of alligators and people have increased the probability and incidence of alligator attacks. Since the 1970s, each attack has been recorded by the Florida Game and Freshwater Fish Commission, and a research programme on alligator attacks has been instituted. More than a dozen alligator attacks a year are now known to have occurred, and while most of the injuries sustained in these attacks were not of a serious nature, a few were, and between 1973 and 1988 six people were killed. In each instance the victim was in the water and was stalked by the alligator, the victim being unaware of the approach of the unpredictable, powerful and hungry predator.

To counter the alligator threat, pugnacious problem animals in densely populated areas are captured by state authorities and moved to areas where the chance of human/alligator interaction is less likely. Given the large number of Floridians and the ever-increasing number of large American alligators in the same area, it is surprising that so few attacks occur. One of the reasons for the relative rarity of attacks is that both male alligators defending their territories and females defending their nest sites give fair warning to intruders by mouth-gaping (an awesome array of teeth), hissing loudly, and assuming a threat display (arching their bodies so that the tail protrudes from the water, and inflating their trunks). However, it is expected that the number will probably grow, as alligators generally show no fear of large animals or humans and, as they become more familiar with humans, the odds on attack will dramatically increase. This is likely to be the case when humans, as is sometimes their tendency, molest or annoy these apparently placid beasts.

Unfortunately, some people tend to treat these big predators as pets and often feed them. There are numerous reports of pet dogs being eaten, a particularly famous one concerning the actress Sarah Bernhardt. Picnicking on the grounds of an American admirer's estate at the end of the last century, Bernhardt was horrified when a log suddenly snapped its head and swallowed her poodle whole. The beast was promptly shot, its head preserved, and the hideous trophy shipped from Florida to Paris where, mounted on a plaque on Bernhardt's drawing-room wall, it continued to disgust and mystify visitors for years. When asked by first-time callers for an explanation of this startling addition to the decor, she would gesture at the grinning jaws, sob and reply: 'My little dog – his tomb!'

*ABOVE:* An American alligator enjoying a large blue crab. Juveniles and young subadults obtain a considerable portion of their calories from invertebrates.

# SIX

# THE
# HUMAN
# HUNTER –
# 70 YEARS
# OF
# DESTRUCTION

Humans are the only large mammals that deliberately hunt crocodilians. This practice goes back to ancient times. In the Cairo Museum there is an exquisite statue of a pharaoh standing on the prow of his boat, spear poised in hand, ready to harpoon a Nile crocodile (*Crocodylus niloticus*). The efficiency of the Ancient Egyptian crocodile hunters is evident at the temples of Kom Ombo in Upper Egypt and Crocodilopolis in Fayoum, where there are large rooms filled with mummified crocodiles of all sizes, stacked one upon another.

*BELOW:* A Roman pavement mosaic from the 2nd century AD shows a scene of human/ crocodilian combat.

# HUMAN-CROCODILIAN CONFLICT

Humans have always been protective of their domestic animals; thus, it comes as no surprise that whenever crocodiles preyed on domestic stock, the human solution was to kill them (the crocodiles). Prior to the introduction of firearms and the commercialization of crocodilian skins, human hunting had relatively little impact on crocodilian populations. But the situation was to change dramatically when rifle-armed hunters were not only

given licences to kill problem crocodiles, but were even paid a bounty by local governments. In German East Africa (Tanzania), one cattle-dealer/hunter killed over 1,600 adult crocodiles in just two months. On the island of Marajo in South America, where the aggressive black cayman (*Melanosuchus niger*) has killed large numbers of domestic cattle, the indigenous people have conducted an annual cayman hunt at the mouth of the Amazon. These hunts have been so successful that the black cayman has nearly been eradicated in that part of the Amazon basin.

## GAMES PEOPLE PLAY

Humans compete with each other in a vast variety of ways and are eager to proclaim their successes by means of trophies. Status used to be achieved by hunting and killing the largest of a species from some exotic land. Although quite an ancient practice, in recent times this form of sport has been limited to the few wealthy and hardy adventurers who could afford such a journey, and to the so-called 'white hunters' who led their safaris and found their prey for them. Interestingly, the sportsman hunter and the white hunter were not responsible for many killings since their main interest was not killing for killing's sake, but in getting their names in the record books and having king-size skins for the walls of their trophy rooms.

The European interest in the Nile crocodile for sport preceded the time of

Christ. Pliny the Elder has described how, in the first century AD, the emperor Nero, to celebrate his Games, ordered the Circus Flaminius to be flooded, where he staged a battle between 36 Nile crocodiles and a party of armed Tentyrites. The animals were slaughtered, and the performance proved to be such a success that it was repeated many times. Today such bloodthirsty sport would generally be considered a disgusting abuse. Although humans have come a long way since then, we still have some way to go: consider, for instance, the number of bulls which are still killed in the bullrings of the world, and the worldwide practice of violent contact sports such as boxing. Crocodiles may take some comfort from the knowledge that they have not been singled out for violent entertainment.

The silliest use of crocodilians in the sports and entertainment field is to be seen in some of the many reptile parks found in Florida and Australia. The sport, alligator-wrestling, pits man against beast as did the Ancient Romans – only in this case the man has no weapons. The goal is to grab the alligator's jaws and hold them shut while rolling the animal on to its back and hypnotizing it by stroking its abdomen. Fortunately for the wrestler, the American alligator is rather mild-mannered, and other than getting knocked end-over-tip by a blow from the alligator's very strong tail, usually no harm comes to either contestant.

*BELOW:* Crocodile farms not only provide skins and meat for sale but also raise adult animals for restocking natural habitats. Part of the expenses of the farms are defrayed by tourism. Here in a farm at Samut Prakan in Thailand, hundreds of tourists watch a local crocodile wrestler show off his skill.

## CAYMANS AND ALLIGATORS AS STUFFED NOVELTIES

Before the sale and importation of stuffed
young caymans and alligators were banned
by law in the United States, hundreds of
thousands of these young crocodilians
were slaughtered, skinned, tanned, stuffed
and fitted with glass eyes. These hapless
reptilian victims were usually 0.5–1.0-m
(1.5–3-ft) long and often mounted in
bizarre positions clothed in outlandish
outfits. They could be purchased in toy
or novelty shops, chain stores, and even
at airport gift shops throughout the
southern states, particularly in Florida
and Louisiana. The appeal of such novel-
ties escapes me, although I remember as a
child receiving two of these grotesque
stuffed animals from relatives returning
from a visit to Florida. I actually became
quite fond of them.

*LEFT:* A Singapore
shop specializing in
crocodilian products
displays its wares. In
this shop alone is
evidence of the
slaughter of
thousands of
animals.

## ALLIGATORS AS A GOURMET FOOD

In many cultures worldwide any protein food is valued, and for many years crocodilians have been hunted purely as a source of meat. Nile crocodile meat has been the main source of protein for one small tribe living on the shores of Lake Turkana in northern Kenya. Despite centuries of hunting, the crocodile population there remained constant, at about 5,000 animals, until the late 1970s when waters were diverted for agricultural purposes. Now, both the hunters and the hunted are in serious decline.

Today, alligators are legally hunted as game and slaughtered as ranched livestock in some parts of Louisiana, where they are a valued food source. An adult alli-

gator provides 20–30 kg (44–66 lb) of meat in its muscular tail. The meat is pinkish-white and, according to those who have eaten it, tastes somewhat like veal or tuna. In Louisiana there is an annual 'gator festival' featuring a variety of 'gator' gourmet specialities such as gator stew, gator meatballs and hot-and-spicy gator Cajun style.

## CROCODILIANS AS PETS

For many years it was fashionable to purchase young caymans and American alligators (*Alligator mississippiensis*) as pets. At the time there was little activity in the animal rights movement (except for dogs and cats), and the young animals were kept and shipped in appalling conditions.

*BELOW:* Appealing though a young American alligator may seem, they are hardly appropriate pets – most will soon die of neglect when kept in such conditions.

It was not uncommon for a pet shop to receive a shipment in which half of the animals were dead and decaying or in such a bad state that they soon died.

Young caymans and alligators are 18–25 cm (7–10 in) long at birth. Because of their long mouths (which appear to be smiling) and their bright eyes, they appeal to many people. They also tend not to bite when they are very young, and do not seem to mind handling. In view of the commercial profits to be made, at one time they were mailed all over the US and the UK. There were even advertising campaigns run by mail-order houses and chain stores to promote the sale of these novel and relatively inexpensive pets.

The majority of alligator and cayman pets usually died of neglect within a few months. Those that did survive grew at the rate of 30 cm (1 ft) a year, and in a couple of years the pet owner was saddled with a metre-long problem. Frequently the pets (particularly the caymans) became more pugnacious and tattooed their owners' hands with neat rows of puncture wounds. In the southern United States, some pet caymans were dumped in ponds, irrigation canals and rivers, where they were able to survive and even establish small breeding populations. Pet owners also tried to get rid of their nippy crocodilians by giving them to animal shelters, zoological societies and schools. In London during the cayman pet heyday (1950s to early 1970s), the London Zoo refused hundreds of requests to accept these poor beasts. They were often released into local rivers and ponds to die of cold. It was not uncommon for dead caymans to be seen floating on the Thames.

The most bizarre means of getting rid of pet alligators was to dump them into the sewers of urban centres such as London and New York City. There was a story in *New Yorker* magazine that described how some of these survived in the sewer waters. Warmed by steam pipes in the sewers and provided with a considerable food supply, ranging from the remnants of discarded pastrami sandwiches to sewer rats, they supposedly grew to considerable size. New York Sewer Department employees were reported to have encountered some of these rather large alligators below the sidewalks of New York. This story, however, turned out to be largely fiction – at least the New York Sewer Department denied it, and in all probability the polluted sewer water hardly provided an adequate environment for growth and survival.

*ABOVE:* Few people would consider keeping a fully grown alligator in their home. Those bought as pets when juveniles are often dumped in the nearest waterways.

RIGHT: Three prime-
quality crocodile
and alligator
pocketbooks such as
these would retail
for about $15,000.
While many skins
sold today are either
from legally hunted
animals or from
commercial farms
and ranches, it is
estimated that at
least a million skins
come from illegal
sources.

# HUNTING CROCODILIANS AS BIG BUSINESS – THE SKINS GAME

Once crocodilian skin was recognized as a source of high-quality, pliable, decorative leather that takes on a bright sheen when processed, trafficking in skins became big business with huge returns. This traffic began in the 1700s when the skins were used to make boots and saddlebags, and continues to this day. Now crocodilian skins are processed into a large variety of very expensive leather products, which are sold in markets around the world. In exclusive shops in Tokyo, Paris, Rome, London, New York, Dallas and Beverly Hills, the purveyors of high fashion promote the sale of crocodilian leather products. The prices are astronomical: a classic skin pocketbook costs $4,000, a coat $9,000, and in Texas one couple paid $30,000 for a matching pair of 'His' and

LEFT: The hunter with the end product, an $8,000 alligator coat. The hunter himself will receive only a few hundred dollars per hide; as the skins pass through middlemen, tanneries, hide suppliers, manufacturers, designers and finally the retailers, each takes a share of the profit.

'Hers' alligator jackets. The customers, usually opulent conspicuous consumers, seek these items as status symbols of their material success, while the retailers promote the products as 'fashion investments'. Such displays are not only in obvious bad taste but are also warrants that ensure the death of thousands of remaining crocodilians. By the early 1900s US tanneries alone were processing between 250,000 and 500,000 skins per year. As supplies dwindled prices rose and so did the profitability of hunting. Even after protective laws were enacted, the profit incentive encouraged large-scale poaching and smuggling of illegal skins by middle-men servicing the tanneries and leather markets.

Given the nature of a supply-and-demand economy, the profitability of hunting by the 1960s had left many species critically threatened. Six species, the American alligator (*Alligator mississippiensis*), the Chinese alligator, (*A. sinensis*), the Orinoco crocodile (*Crocodylus intermedius*), the Cuban crocodile (*C. rhombifer*), the American crocodile (*C. acutus*) and the Indopacific crocodile (*C. porosus*), were on the verge of extinction in the wild. Hunters using aircraft to reach remote, previously unexploited areas brought back skins of species which previously had been inaccessible. Today the world market for crocodilian skins is about two million hides per year. Some of these come from licensed, controlled

*BELOW:* Because of the extent of hunting that has been conducted until recently, the Chinese alligator has been brought dangerously close to extinction.

hunting and some are harvested from the captive populations on farms and ranches. These skins are considered to be legal, but at least a million of the hides taken annually are obtained from poachers.

In today's market untanned hides bring the poacher about $160 per metre for a classic, high-quality skin. Thus, a 2.5-m (8-ft) adult crocodile will bring in about $400. On the other hand, the bony skins of the South American cayman, which make a less pliable, rough leather, obtained from local poachers may cost only $10 for the entire hide. At least 70% of the skins coming to the tanners come from caymans.

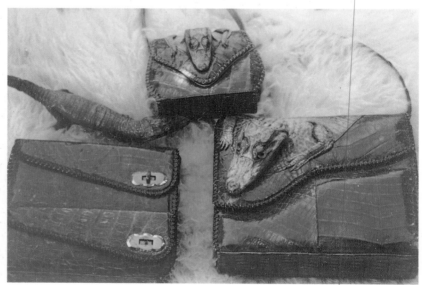

These illegal hides enter the skins game network by being laundered. For example, Brazil has an absolute ban on hunting and exporting game products; however, its neighbour states Bolivia and Paraguay do permit export of skins. The end result is that huge numbers of skins poached in Brazil are smuggled out by commercial hunters, often using the same tactics and routes of transport as drug smugglers. These skins are then purchased by middlemen before being sold to the tanneries for processing. This is where the laundering occurs, as legal skins and poached skins are pooled by middlemen. Although illegal, the incentive for profit is so great that this procedure is widely practised. After the tanners have added their profit margin to the overall cost, the hides are shipped to major leather centres, New York being the main customer, followed by Italy and France. Although importation of illegal skins is banned, identification of species from a tanned

hide is difficult, and there is a real shortage of trained inspectors at the points of entry. Once the hides reach the manufacturer, *haute couture* designers practise their art, add their fees to the profit chain and ship them off to exclusive shops, where the price is increased by at least 200%. So the end result is very expensive indeed.

Another cause of crocodilian population depletion is the airport market for tourists travelling in developing countries. Here, local hunters supply skins which have been inexpertly processed to be made into bargain novelty items and native handicrafts. These items are relatively inexpensive and serve either as mementoes of a vacation or as gifts for the family and neighbours at home. Often these skin products come from endangered species, are of inferior workmanship, are poorly tanned and may even smell or carry infectious diseases. Some of the products are grotesque and include the animals' head and feet.

ABOVE: Once
abundant
throughout the Nile,
the Nile crocodile is
now limited in
numbers, and found
only south of the
fourth cataract. This
Nile crocodile has a
research radio fixed
to its head to
monitor its
movements.

## HUNTING TECHNIQUES

The larger skins bringing the greatest profit used to be found in the bigger and more accessible bodies of water. Hunters in motor-powered boats and armed with high-powered rifles found crocodiles, caymans and alligators easy game. Often they were 'jacked', which means that they were hunted with spotlights at night because the tapetum lucidum of the crocodile's eyes reflects a bright, yellow-orange glow when light is shone upon it. As the larger specimens were depleted by European hunters, the middlemen for the tanneries recruited indigenous people to keep up the supply of skins. Often they were poor peasants who could make more money from hunting crocodiles, caymans

and gharyals than they ever imagined. To compensate for a lack of reliable firearms and expensive ammunition, they devised a number of highly effective hunting procedures. The most ancient of these involved the use of spears and harpoons or large, baited hooks. In India some opportunistic hunters during the dry season invaded the dens of aestivating crocodiles, roping them and pulling them out. Others engaged in the potentially dangerous tactic of diving to the bottoms of salt lakes to rope large mugger crocodiles (*Crocodylus palustris*) resting on the bottom.

In Australia the Indopacific crocodile population was reduced from a quarter of a million to only a few thousand in less than 70 years. The Nile crocodile used to be found in small numbers in what is now called Israel and was abundant for the entire course of the Nile, but by the end of World War I they had disappeared from Palestine and were absent beyond the second cataract of the Nile. In present-day Botswana's Okavango swamp, one hunter earned in excess of $100,000 a year selling skins of slaughtered crocodiles. Everywhere where large crocodilians were to be found the story was the same: mass slaughter to the verge of extinction. It was not only male hunters who killed for cash; sometimes the killing was in aid of a higher purpose. For example, there was a Catholic nun in New Guinea who, seeking funds to help raise a church at her mission, killed and sold skins of the rare, long-snouted New Guinea crocodile (*Crocodylus novaeguineae*), a species tottering on the brink of extinction.

It is estimated that at the turn of the century the leather market consumed over 250,000 alligator skins a year. By 1929 the killing continued at almost the same levels, but by then the populations were depleted. By 1939 only 18,000 skins were taken, and by 1943 only 6,800 alligator hides were sold. With the depletion of supply the price per 2-m (7-ft) hide increased from $4 to almost $20, thus increasing the incentive for further hunting. In the 1960s the state of Florida passed its first law to protect the state animal, the 'gator', and banned the taking of specimens under 1.2 m (4 ft). In other states outright legal bans on alligator hunting were enacted to prevent the extinction of this valuable, endangered reptilian. Today, throughout the southern United States the populations of alligators have recovered so significantly that controlled hunting is once again permitted.

The Indopacific or saltwater crocodiles of northern Australia have also suffered severe losses to skin hunters. Prior to the arrival of Europeans, the crocodile population in the Northern Territory exceeded 250,000 individuals, but by the 1970s the salties were on the verge of extinction. However, today it is estimated that about 56,000 wild salties exist and that another 7,500 are being reared on crocodile ranches and farms.

## COMPETITION BETWEEN HUMANS AND CROCODILIANS

The human population explosion is the ultimate threat to the crocodilians because our voracious quest for land (for commerce, recreation and housing) inevitably encroaches on and destroys more and

*BELOW:* Saltwater crocodiles at the crocodile farm in Sandakan. Many of the adults on farms are problem animals captured in the wild and thus not only cease to pose a threat but can also be used as breeding stock.

more natural habitat. In Florida, people need not only land but also water for drinking and agriculture. In the not-too-distant past water in southern Florida was plentiful, draining from Lake Okeechobee southward as far as the Everglades, a 113-km (70-mile)-wide, shallow, swampy river only a few metres deep. This was an ideal alligator habitat that supported huge numbers of prey, but as pressures for development and water needs increased, canals were dug, dikes and dams were constructed, and a large part of the former swamp was drained. Much of the alligators' natural habitat is now occupied by housing projects, marinas, golf courses, shopping malls and industrial areas.

With the destruction of much of their ecosystem, it is not surprising to learn that alligators are now frequently showing up in canals and in ponds on golf courses. They are losing their fear of humans and, with the decline of their natural food sources, are becoming a major predator of human pets. With the increased human/alligator interaction there is pressure to capture and remove 'problem' animals. Although there are new and promising methods for management of both land and water use in southern Florida, the alligator population there remains under pressure.

In northern Australia a similar phenomenon is evident. The Northern Territory that once was only sparsely settled has experienced a significant increase in human inhabitants. During World War II the 'top end' of Australia had only 20,000 residents, but today there are not only over 150,000 permanent residents but also, because of tourist promotion over 300,000 tourists flock to this previously unspoiled land each year. Similarly, the population of nearby Queensland is growing rapidly (about 2.5 million), and many of their developments are encroaching on the habitat of both the salt-water crocodile and the Australian freshwater crocodile (*Crocodylus johnsoni*).

And so it goes all over the world – particularly in India, Africa and Central and South America, where the human population has literally exploded. In Kenya the population is growing at more than 5% per year, and the pressure on crocodilian habitats is severe. More and more dams are being built, waters are being diverted for agricultural developments, and bigger doses of pollutants are entering the aquatic environment. Adding to the

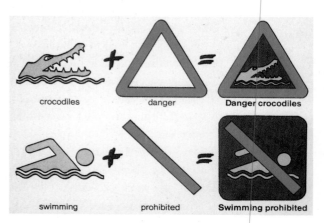

*BELOW:* With an increasing local population and more tourists coming to northern Australia, there is an urgent need to alert people to the dangers of crocodiles, as this sign in a Queensland national park suggests.

toll of crocodilian deaths is the slaughter caused by commercial fishermen whose nets entrap crocodiles and haryials, causing them to suffocate. Even in developed nations with stringent protective laws, there are new threats posed by the propellors of high-speed boats and (on land) by increased traffic. About half of the deaths recorded for adults of the closely monitored populations of American crocodile (*Crocodylus acutus*) were due to accidents involving motor vehicles.

# SEVEN

# THE
# HUMAN
# CONSERVATOR:
# PROTECTING
# THE
# ENDANGERED

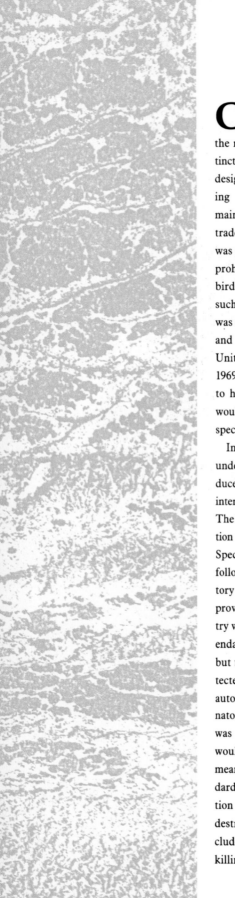

Once humans had begun to realize that the crocodilians, the last of the ruling reptiles, were in danger of extinction, they started to institute measures designed to protect their ever-diminishing populations. It was clear that the main cause of their depletion was the skin trade and, as early as 1900, the Lacey Act was passed in the United States. This act prohibited interstate commerce of wild birds and mammals and their products, such as skins and feathers. Later, the act was expanded to include fish, amphibians and reptiles, and eventually became the United States Endangered Species Act of 1969. Part of this act called upon the US to host an international conference that would write an international endangered species treaty.

In 1973 81 nations gathered together under United Nations auspices to produce an agreement that would govern international trade in endangered species. The treaty, known as CITES (Convention on International Trade in Endangered Species), went into force in 1973 with the following stipulations: that each signatory nation would agree to enforce the provisions of the treaty; that each country would decide which of its species were endangered and which not endangered but threatened; and that any species protected by one signatory nation would automatically be protected by other signatory nations. Also written into the act was the understanding that each nation would monitor its wildlife populations by means of accurate studies, whose standards included gathering data on population size, range, habitat and sources of destruction. Sources of destruction included poaching, hunting, accidental killing and habitat destruction. In addi-

tion, basic studies on behaviour, reproduction, ecology and physiology were to be undertaken.

It soon became apparent that not very much was known about crocodilians. Being large and dangerous, and often inhabiting remote areas, research lagged, but in time a small, dedicated group of crocodilian investigators emerged. At the same time a small group of impassioned conservationists at zoological parks around the world embarked on controlled captive breeding programmes to ensure the preservation of endangered species. They were joined by other conservationists from national park services around the world, and all three groups contributed to form the Crocodile Specialist Group under the aegis of the International Union for the Conservation of Nature and Natural Resources (IUCN), which also publishes a list of endangered species. It is thanks to this small cadre of workers, with the help of enlightened politicians (and even commercial skin traders in many nations), that there is hope that all 22 extant species of crocodilians will be saved.

## ENFORCING THE TREATY

Many nations worldwide have set aside vast areas of natural habitat for national parks and game reserves, and have established game departments to monitor licensed hunting. In the wealthier nations significant resources have been dedicated to the enforcement of protective laws. At the federal level in the United States, the US Fish and Wildlife Agency, along with rangers of the National Park Service and Forestry Service, provided effective protection, which was later augmented by other state agencies that regulated hunting

THE HUMAN
CONSERVATOR:
PROTECTING
THE
ENDANGERED

111

*ABOVE:* Radio tracking Nile crocodiles on Lake Ngezi, Zimbabwe. Such studies are an essential part of the CITES agreement to protect vanishing species.

in state parks with their own rangers and game wardens. Many of these states, realizing that many endangered species represented a valuable source of revenue and tourism, were particularly diligent, and some have been very effective, for example the Fish and Game Departments of Florida and Louisiana. Some of these efforts were sponsored in part by governments and in part by conservation-oriented philanthropists, who set aside large tracts of land on which crocodilians could be bred and studied.

In Australia both federal and local efforts have been particularly effective. In the Northern Territory the previously endangered Australian freshwater crocodile (*Crocodylus johnsoni*) and the Indopacific crocodile (*C. porosus*) were brought back from the edge of extinction to a point

where they could be removed from CITES I and placed in CITES II, which permits carefully limited harvesting from existing natural populations. In the United States the American alligator (*Alligator mississipiensis*) population also showed such a dramatic recovery in some locations that it created a nuisance. These animals too are now listed in CITES II, and controlled hunting is permitted.

In developing nations similar events have transpired. Laws have been enacted and vast areas of land set aside for the creation of national parks under the protection of game wardens and park rangers. However, these nations are poor and, despite some funding provided by various governments and conservation organizations, the enforcement of protective laws ranges from nominal to totally ineffectual.

When buying crocodilian products, it is possible to detect whether one is being offered a lower quality cayman skin labelled as genuine alligator. The distinct differences between each type of hide will become evident on close inspection, and are shown in the details of skin types here.

## CLOSE-UP COMPARISON OF CROCODILIAN SKINS

A  Alligator skin is smooth and without sensory pits.
B  Detail of alligator skin: sometimes the hide will include the area around the umbilicus, which has a spider's web appearance.
C  Crocodile hides are similar to alligator hides, but have sensory pits.
D  Cayman skins have fissures and pits on each scale.

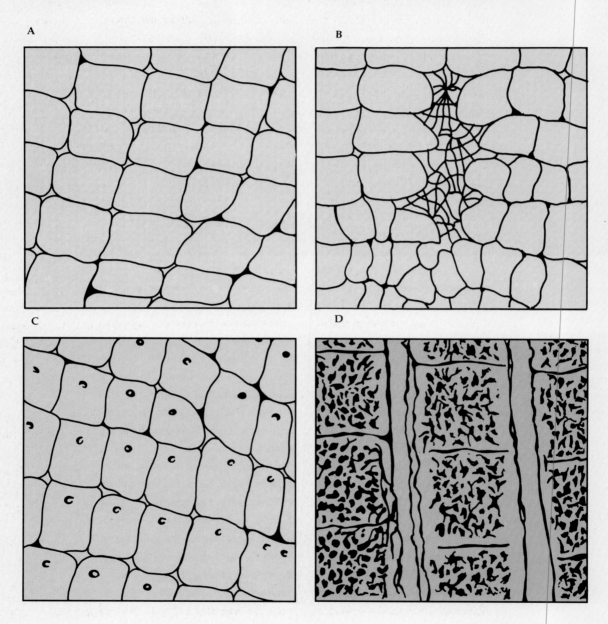

There are several reasons for this break-down: first, the numbers of rangers are limited in terms of the size of the districts to be covered; and, second, their salaries are small, the latter producing an incentive for corruption. While corruption is not the exclusive domain of the poorer nations, it is practised with a vengeance at all levels in some of the developing nations. In Kenya not only are the park rangers spread thinly but also there have been cases in which the rangers, wardens and government officials were all actively involved in the poaching and sale of products from protected species. Fortunately, international pressure on local governments has limited some of these abuses, particularly in African nations and in India, where tourism in national parks brings in considerable income in much needed foreign exchange.

Another problem of enforcement occurs at the sites of export and at the import customs desks. Several countries didn't sign CITES or, if they did, they don't do much to enforce the regulations. In New York City, where 80% of all crocodilian skins are shipped, there are fewer than two dozen inspectors available to monitor trade in wildlife products. Elsewhere it is worse, and there have been many reports of corrupt customs officials turning a blind eye on illegal exports.

Another factor making enforcement difficult is the unceasing organization of illegal poaching. In Kenya a recent incident details the problem. In Marsabit, a park in the north, a small population of rhinoceroses was introduced. Poachers from Somalia, equipped with four-wheel drive vehicles, chain saws and AK-47 assault rifles, attacked the rangers' headquarters, overcoming them easily as the

rangers' old, bolt-action Enfields were no match for the poachers' automatic weapons. Meanwhile, another group of poachers went out and killed the rhinoceroses, harvested their horns and then escaped across the border.

In South America Brazil tries to protect its crocodilians inhabiting the vast Amazon basin, but well-financed hunters fly in, devastate the crocodilian populations and then fly their ill-gotten skins to neighbouring countries that are not CITES signatories. This particular kind of problem is the most perplexing one for conservationists. Enforcement of hunting regulations is gradually improving, but countries such as Paraguay, Bolivia and Colombia turn a blind eye, allowing smugglers working through middlemen to launder illegal hides, often with the complicity of corrupt tannery officials. Once tanned and mixed with legally acquired skins, they are difficult to detect. The manufacturer is often duped as are the retailers and consumers.

The highest-quality hides come from the sides and belly of American alligators (*Alligator mississippiensis*), followed by the hides of Nile and Indopacific crocodiles (*Crocodylus niloticus* and *C. porosus*), which are considered classic skins and are the most expensive. The horn-belly skins of the lower-quality, cheap South American caymans are often sold at a premium price as genuine alligator or crocodile. Indeed, most of the two million skins used every year come from caymans. An educated consumer doesn't believe either the sales pitch of the retailer or the stamped label. If the skin is smooth, soft and glossy and devoid of pits it is a genuine American alligator hide. In some cases the skin from around the alligator's umbilicus produces

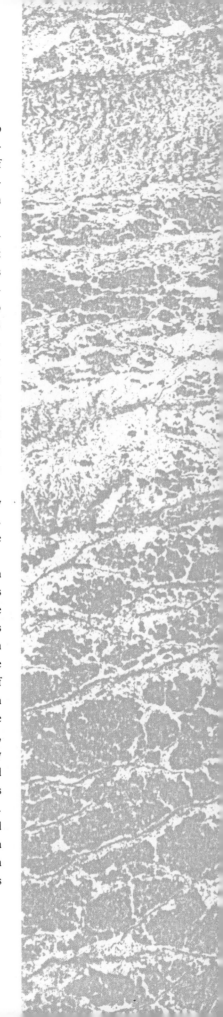

a weblike pattern. Crocodile hides are similar but have one or two sensory pits. Unfortunately, one cannot tell whether the crocodile skin came from a legally harvested animal. Cayman skins have fissures and pits on each scale, and the poorest-quality skins have a hump of bone projecting from the surface of each scale.

## EDUCATION PROGRAMME

While enforcement of protective laws is critical, so is public education, particularly in areas where crocodilian attacks on humans are exploited by sensationalist media coverage, such as 'Croc Took My Dad'. Such tabloid headlines create public hysteria and calls for elimination of the animals wherever human/crocodilian interactions occur. The Australian govern-

ment has dealt with this problem in two ways. First, instead of shooting suspected man-killers, it has instituted, like the United States, a programme to capture the beasts and ship them to commercial ranches. Capturing a one-tonne, 6.4-m (21-ft) armoured animal with an aggressive disposition is not easy but can be done. The second was the development of a long-overdue public education programme.

A first step in such a programme was to erect signs warning the public in areas where Indopacific crocodiles encroach on human recreational areas. The Conservation Commission sent its rangers to schools to teach children how to avoid attack, and television and radio programmes reached a very wide audience. The ranching programme also helps improve the image of Australian crocodiles since their potential for bringing

*BELOW:* This gharial displays growth indicator marks; it is part of a breeding study being undertaken in Nepal.

in foreign exchange and benefiting local economies is a great aid to inducing the public to view crocodiles in a more benign light. The newly enlightened public attitude towards the spike-toothed voracious 'salties' was seen in a recent incident in which two swimmers were attacked and eaten. Instead of a wave of shooting, the public left the problem crocodile to the authorities, whose attitude was that anyone swimming in a river full of big crocodiles was literally asking for trouble.

## CONSERVATION IN INDIA

In India as early as 2000 BC the concept of conservation was introduced in the Hindu precept of Ahimsa which preached non-violence towards any living organism. Shortly after this the Emperor Ashoka issued history's first conservation law. In the eighteenth century, with the rise of colonialism, hunting for sport dramatically increased, but it wasn't until 1947, when independence came, that the newly liberated population, freed from the shooting regulations of the despised colonialists, launched a campaign of wholesale slaughter throughout the sub-continent. It was a war against the animals, and populations of the once-sacred mugger crocodile (*Crocodylus palustris*), the Indopacific crocodile and the great long-nosed gharyal (*Gavialis gangeticus*) suffered huge losses. Along with this post-war bloodletting there was widespread habitat destruction to make way for new grazing grounds, agricultural development, dam building and creation of industrial centres, all to meet the needs of an expanding human population.

In 1969 the International Union for Conservation of Nature and Natural

Resources met in New Delhi and highlighted the problem. The late Prime Minister Indira Ghandi addressed the convention and gave it her endorsement. This was followed by the enactment of protective laws under the 1972 Indian Wildlife Protection Act. Monies were contributed by the government and the World Wildlife Fund. One hundred and fifty new national parks and sanctuaries were established. In some areas foresters and rangers have been effective in stopping the slaughter while in other areas law enforcement is minimal or non-existent. The biggest problem is the growth of the human population, which creates enormous pressures on the parks. 'People or animals?' ask the impoverished Indians. After all, the price of one poached mugger hide could feed a family for a year. One pessimistic scientist summed it up by saying that all that would be left by the turn of the twenty-first century would be what was left in their native preserves. But now things are being done that could affect the future of the endangered Indian resident crocodiles.

*ABOVE:* Breeding projects such as this Nepalese study base are essential to reintroduce a controlled number of crocodilians into the wild and replenish the natural gene pool.

ABOVE: One of the most successful conservation efforts originated in India's Madras Crocodile Bank.

BELOW: This farm in Zariba, Zimbabwe, raises Nile crocodiles for profit and provides a reserve population for restocking depleted natural habitats.

FACING PAGE, ABOVE: A researcher demonstrates how research radios are fixed to the heads of Nile crocodiles to monitor their habits.

FACING PAGE, BELOW: Collecting eggs for incubation ensures that a greater percentage of the eggs hatch.

In 1971 at the first IUCN meeting the crocodile specialist group decided to establish a crocodile bank in which the gene pool of endangered crocodilians could be preserved. This led to the creation of the Madras Crocodile Bank. Financing for the project came from many sources, including the West German Reptile Leather Association. The goals of the bank were not only to breed animals in captivity but also to produce enough of them to supply other breeding centres and to provide sufficient animals to the Indian government to restock previously depleted populations. Today there are over 3,600 animals in the bank, including American and African species. The operation of this research and breeding centre, which covers 3.4 ha (8.5 acres), is funded by grants from the National Geographic Society, the Smithsonian Institution and many other conservation-oriented agencies, as well as from fees paid by the half-million visitors who pass through each year.

A fundamental component of any conservation effort involves public education programmes which heighten awareness, and the Madras Crocodile Bank has produced a number of publications and films towards this end. In fact, this particular bank, with its reintroduction programme under the leadership of Singh and Whittaker, has been used as a model by other developing countries for their crocodilian conservation programmes. Today, the restocking programme is well under way. Hopefully, the potentiality for future commercial development of the depleted populations will serve as an incentive to the Indian government to manage this renewable resource with vigour.

## CONSERVATION IN AFRICA

Commercial hunting of the Nile crocodile throughout Africa had, by the 1960s, so depleted natural populations that some governments began to enact legislation to prevent or at least limit hunting and set aside vast, relatively remote areas as national parks. Unfortunately, not all governments enforced the laws, and other countries openly violated them by taking poached hides from neighbouring countries and exporting them. In some areas the instability of some of these newly liberated countries led to civil wars and, in Uganda's Murchison Falls Park, site of one major population of Nile crocodiles, teenage rebels armed with automatic assault weapons wantonly slaughtered most of that population.

With the commercial value of crocodilian hides increasing, the government of Zimbabwe saw the opportunity for increasing the input of foreign exchange, and in 1965 sponsored two crocodile

ranches.

By 1988 the farming effort in Africa had not only increased to 10 ranches in Zimbabwe but also had spread to Kenya, Tanzania, Zambia, Madagascar and South Africa. Many of these ranches and farms, in order to obtain a licence, must agree that they will provide a certain number of immature crocodiles for reintroduction into the wild.

In the setting up of these ranches, many technical problems had to be ironed out, from egg collecting and incubation methods to minimizing mortality among the hatchlings. These problems have largely been solved.

The farms also developed a variety of diets that allow the young to thrive and grow more rapidly than they would in the wild, reaching harvesting size in two to three years. After skinning, the meat from the harvested animals is recycled to the cannibalistic young crocodiles in the rearing yards. Once the good belly leather has been shipped to tanners, the backskins and heads are sold to locals for the curio trade. It is estimated that a ranch, if it is to be successful, has to produce at least 2,000 skins per year. This means a viable operation must have up to 100 adult, breeding females. These animals come from wild populations, often from areas of high density. Also, in the past, problem crocodiles (that is, man-eaters and cattle-eaters) were shot out of hand. Today they are captured and shipped to farms and ranches.

One advantage of African skin farming is that it has reduced crocodile poaching, although some still goes on. These farms, being dependent on the wild populations, have also sponsored some research projects of their own.

## CONSERVATION IN SOUTH AMERICA AND CENTRAL AMERICA

Among the most severely threatened species is the magnificent, long-snouted Orinoco crocodile (*Crocodylus intermedius*) found only in the middle and lower reaches of the Orinoco River basin. When the explorer Alexander von Humboldt first penetrated this region, he wrote vivid accounts of encounters with huge numbers of animals, many measuring over 6 m (20 ft) in length. Although the local populace had long hunted these animals, which they considered a threat both to humans and to cattle, it was not until the 1930s that exploitation for their skins began in earnest. Hunters, the 'caimaneros', first devastated easily accessible populations and then moved farther upriver and into lesser tributaries. By the 1950s the plunder had so depleted the numbers of Orinoco crocodiles that hunting was no longer commercially feasible, but the remaining populations failed to recover.

ABOVE: A crocodile wrestler displays his skills in a test of strength.

RIGHT: The Samut Prakan Crocodile Farm in Thailand has been vital to the regeneration of the endangered Siamese crocodile.

In 1978 the first organized conservation programme began under the directorship of FUDENA, Fundacion para la Defensa de la Naturaleza. It was an essential first step to determine how many Orinoco crocodiles remained, where they lived and what their habitat requirements were. This survey was brought up to date in 1986 in a countrywide study using aerial searches, boat searches and interviews, but was complicated by the fact that the spectacled cayman (*Caiman crocodylus*), another large but unendangered (though vulnerable) crocodilian, shared its range. It was found that a few small populations of Orinoco crocodiles, numbering less than 1,000 in total, existed in scattered localities. It was also found that pollution, agricultural irrigation projects and other human endeavours were severely disrupting their natural habitat and that Orinoco crocodile populations were still declining.

As early as 1984, a wealthy Venezuelan conservationist established a captive breeding centre on his ranch. A crocodilian specialist, Dr Thorb Janarson, joined him and, with the support of FUDENA, the World Wide Fund for Nature, the World Wildlife Fund and the New York Zoological Society, they began a modest captive population programme with the aim of producing and rearing juvenile Orinoco crocodiles for eventual reintroduction into their former habitats. This required not only the development of captive breeding technology but also studies of the ecology of their natural environment. It was also clear that no reintroduction programme could be effective without a commitment from the Venezuelan government.

Husbandry included breeding captive animals and collecting and incubating eggs taken from nests in the wild where eggs suffer high mortality due to nest-raiding by Tegu lizards and hungry people. The current breeding programme now has about 100 juveniles being reared in captivity until they grow big enough to reintroduce into the wild. Reintroduction will follow the successful programme that Singh and Whittaker devised for India, a programme that demanded protection of natural habitats. In 1988 the Venezuelan government established a new national park whose boundaries include large sections of river ideal for Orinoco crocodile

reintroduction. In 1989 reintroduction began in this park. Plans are currently under way to increase the productivity of breeding centres, and new areas are being examined for their potential as future restocking sites.

As of today only Venezuela, of all the South American countries, has an established crocodilian management programme. Its success will depend on how well the law enforcement programme functions in the face of population pressure on the parks. Fortunately, commercial interests have a stake in seeing the programme work, and tanners and ranchers have funded a new conservation group to help in the preservation of both the Orinoco and American crocodiles. Ironically, this programme is partially supported by funds derived from the sale of legally hunted caymans.

In the Caribbean the Cuban government has enacted laws to protect crocodilians in the Zapata swamp, the Lanier swamp and on the Isla de Pinos. However, in the wild the endangered Cuban crocodile (*C. rhombifer*) has hybridized with the American crocodile (*C. acutus*), and also finds itself in competition with the spectacled cayman, which was introduced into the Lanier swamp as a commercial venture. In addition to the wild populations, thousands of crocodiles are held in captivity on government-sponsored farms where recently an attempt was made to separate out old, unhybridized Cuban crocodiles in order to produce a genetically pure stock. This was not easy since the Cuban crocodile in captivity develops an exceptionally aggressive disposition.

## CROCODILE FARMING IN SOUTH-EAST ASIA

Just south of Bangkok lies the Samut Prakan Crocodile Farm, which has over 30,000 Siamese (*C. siamensis*) and Indopacific crocodiles kept in huge, open-air pools. This farm has been instrumental in helping to save the endangered Siamese crocodile. It not only makes a profit from the sale of hides and other products but also is a major tourist attraction.

In New Guinea, after a modest start on small farms, ranching has become big business. A company called Mainland Holding, in cooperation with the government, has established a large commercial ranch with close to 30,000 animals, small and large, in stock. Such a large popula-

tion of voracious eaters requires a considerable food supply, and this is provided by the ranch's own chicken farm that produces enough poultry to support up to 40,000 crocodilians. All animals on the farm are the property of the Conservator of Fauna, who controls licensing and can, if need be, direct the ranch to reintroduce animals back into the wild.

## CONSERVATION OF THE AMERICAN CROCODILE

The northernmost range of any crocodile is the southernmost tip of Florida where a small, well-protected population of American crocodiles (*C. acutus*) exists. The transformed natural landscape that limited their range now supports about 500 animals. A 15-year study of subadult and adult deaths indicated that the demise of 27 of these animals was primarily due to motor vehicles, followed by wanton shooting. In order to protect these endangered animals, education programmes have been made which point out that this animal, though large and fearsome in appearance, is really quite passive and does not attack humans. Habitats have been protected by both state and federal agencies as well as by the nuclear power industry.

Nuclear-powered electrical generating stations are cooled by circulating water around their hot cores. This effluent water is both hot and very slightly radioactive. These plants are also restricted areas where human trespass is limited; because of this, both American crocodiles and alligators have found havens in some of these protected areas. In southern Florida the major nuclear power plant, at Turkey Point, has found increasing numbers of

endangered American crocodiles in residence and even successfully breeding in the 270-km (168-mile) network of mangrove-lined cooling canals. Given the negative attitude of some people towards nuclear power, the Florida Power and Light Company, realizing that its public image would be enhanced by efforts to save an endangered species, has spent hundreds of thousands of dollars in a crocodile research effort. Today about 20 adults and some subadults thrive there, enjoying a degree of protection and privacy. Plans for expansion of the nuclear facilities have been abandoned, and the crocodile habitat is safe for the foreseeable future, at least.

In the heyday of the Savannah River Atomic Production facility, five production reactors were running at maximum output to make weapons-grade plutonium for atomic bombs and tritium for hydrogen bombs. The boiling-hot, slightly radioactive coolant water was channelled into a large artificial lake where it was cooled by evaporative heat loss and then recycled as a coolant. Needless to say the security around the 777-sq-km (300-sq-mile) atomic facility was very tight, and as a result the small crocodile population indigenous to the area enjoyed a population boom. The crocodiles thrived because their protected habitat was devoid of hunters and because there was a huge population of very large bass in the coolant lake. The Savannah River Ecology Laboratory, under the direction of the University of Georgia, has been studying this resident breeding population of more than 100 adult American crocodiles.

Other efforts to preserve the small American wild crocodile population include live trapping of egg predators such

as the raccoon in nesting areas. There have also been some reintroduction efforts from captured foreign populations, but since these might be very different genetically from the local population, such efforts are now deemed inappropriate. A more beneficial effort involves collecting eggs from nests in the wild, incubating and hatching them and rearing the captive young for subsequent release. The major benefit of this type of programme is that the normally high mortality rate of eggs and hatchlings can be short-circuited. There are also efforts to maintain captive breeding programmes which serve as a buffer should some sort of catastrophe befall the natural populations. Captive breeding efforts are discussed later in this chapter.

## AUSTRALIAN COMMERCIAL FARMS AND RANCHES

The first crocodile farm in Australia was established in 1969 to protect small, wild Indopacific crocodiles (*C. porosus*) from becoming curios. Its initial efforts were a failure until the mid-1970s when it was

*ABOVE:* There are only about 500 American crocodiles left in the southern tip of Florida. While they are carefully protected, a number have been killed by automobiles. The park service has now posted warning signs at known crocodile crossing areas.

developed into an on-site commercial breeding farm. This farm, like all its successors, was rigidly regulated and had to comply with all governmental and international guidelines. Today there are seven ranches holding both the Indopacific crocodile and the Australian freshwater crocodile (*C. johnsoni*). These ranches, often funded by governmental agencies, are also used as captive breeding facilities to provide animals for restocking. They provide a source of employment for locals and serve as tourist attractions, too. The main profit is, of course, from high-quality hides, but crocodile meat is also marketed in ever-increasing amounts. There are thousands of animals currently on the farms, and the industry is on the verge of self-sufficiency.

## AQUARIUM AND ZOOLOGICAL GARDEN CAPTIVE BREEDING PROGRAMMES

In the past 20 years the technology of breeding captive crocodilians has improved to the point where all of the endangered species are being bred in small but increasing numbers. In the United States a number of zoos have been particularly successful.

Even institutions in harsh, cold climates have created indoor facilities in which breeding is intensively managed. One noteworthy effort is that of the Bronx Zoo in New York under the direction of John Behler. The most important breedings to date have been of the critically endangered Chinese alligator (*Alligator sinensis*) and Cuban crocodile (*Crocodylus rhombifer*). In the warmer parts of the United States where outdoor space is available, the St Augustine Alligator Farm in Florida and its subsidiary in California at Ocala have bred nine different species. The zoo in Atlanta has had great success in breeding Morelet's crocodile (*C. moreletii*), and the Miami Metro Zoo has bred both Siamese crocodiles (*C. siamensis*) and the African slender-snouted crocodile (*C. cataphractus*).

In Fort Worth, Texas, they are successfully breeding African dwarf crocodiles (*Osteolaemus tetraspis*), and in Washington DC, Cuban crocodiles are being propagated. In Albuquerque, New Mexico, scientists are raising Cuvier's dwarf caymans, and in Cincinnati, Ohio, smooth-fronted (Schneider's dwarf) caymans. Clearly, zoological parks and aquaria will play a major role in conserving highly endangered crocodilians. These breedings are summarized in John Behler's report, *Status, Captive Culture and Crocodilian Advising Group Recommendation*, in the 1989 American Association of Zoo Management (AAZM) Proceedings. I have presented some of this report in tabular form with his kind permission; this appears on the following page.

*BELOW:* Crocodile farms require a copious source of food to take care of the voracious appetites of their residents. Some farms use poultry and have their own poultry farms. Others use fish, as seen in this farm at Vayapura in Irian Jaya.

*ABOVE:* The Bronx Zoo facility was created at great expense and although much of the background vegetation is artificial, it appears very realistic to those on the walkways overlooking the exhibit. The bright spots in the water are coins thrown by visitors; some of the exhibit animals have become ill from swallowing coins with a high zinc content.

| Endangered Species | Successful Breeding by |
|---|---|
| **CHINESE ALLIGATOR** *(Alligator sinensis)* | Joint Project Bronx Zoo and Rockefeller Wildlife Refuge in Louisiana. Also Bronx Zoo, St Augustine Farm, Shanghai Zoo. |
| **SPECTACLED OR COMMON CAYMAN** *(Caiman crocodylus)* | Atlanta Zoo, Dominican Republic National Zoo, Busch Gardens in Florida. |
| **AFRICAN SLENDER-SNOUTED CROCODILE** *(Crocodylus cataphractus)* | Miami Metro Zoo. |
| **ORINOCO CROCODILE** *(Crocodylus intermedius)* | No success in zoos but some on private ranches. |
| **AUSTRALIAN FRESHWATER CROCODILE** *(Crocodylus johnsoni)* | Although listed in CITES I, breeding is going on in the Melbourne Zoo. Thousands on farms and ranches. |
| **PHILIPPINE CROCODILE** *(Crocodylus mindorensis)* | Sillinian University on Negros in Philippine Islands. No breeding to date. |
| **MORELET'S CROCODILE** *(Crocodylus moreletii)* | Breeds readily, Atlanta Zoo, Tuxtla Gutierrez Zoo in Chiapas. |
| **MUGGER OR MARSH CROCODILE** *(Crocodylus palustris)* | The Madras Crocodile Bank Trust has been very successful in breeding this broad-snouted crocodile, as have a number of Indian zoos. |
| **INDOPACIFIC CROCODILE** *(Crocodylus porosus)* | Despite its size and mean temperament, is being bred in zoos in Djafa, Singapore and Higashi, and thousands are being bred on farms and ranches in New Guinea and Australia. |
| **CUBAN CROCODILE** *(Crocodylus rhombifer)* | Captive breeding in Bronx Zoo, Washington DC Zoo and Stockholm, as well as on American alligator farms. |
| **SIAMESE CROCODILE** *(Crocodylus siamensis)* | Large populations in zoos, and on farms and ranches. |
| **FALSE GHARYAL** *(Tomistoma schlegelii)* | Bred in Bronx and Miami Zoos and farmed in Thailand. |
| **GHARYAL** *(Gavialis gangeticus)* | Farm breeding programmes in India have thousands ready for restocking. Few breeding in zoos such as Nan da Kan Biological Park in India. |

## THE STUD BOOK

One major problem in rearing animals in limited numbers from the same breeding stock is the loss of genetic diversity. It is well known that inbreeding produces less viable animals, and in all breeding programmes for endangered species, attempts are made to keep accurate breeding records and maintain diversity. To this end the Crocodilian Advisory Group (CAG) of the American Association of Zoological Parks and Aquaria have produced recommendations and directions to limit this problem. These recommendations not only involve the creation of special survival plans but also the maintenance of a crocodilian stud book by which lineages of zoo-bred offspring can be genetically managed.

*ABOVE:* A major attraction for tourists is the extensive American alligator farm at Saint Augustine, Florida. This lavish ranch not only attracts hundreds of thousands of tourists, but its facilities have been used by a number of researchers to study crocodilian behaviour.

# EIGHT

# THE
# FUTURE
# FOR
# CROCODILIANS

**ABOVE:** This shot of massed American alligators in an alligator farm in Florida belies the very real danger of extinction that now faces most species of crocodilians.

Crocodilians and humans share several common characteristics. Both show a high degree of parental guardianship. Both have very long lifespans with individuals reaching ages of up to 100 years. Both hunt each other and are very efficient predators. However, crocodilians rely on a hunting strategy and technique that have remained the same for 190 million years, while humans have developed tools and weapons that can strike at long range with deadly efficiency. The balance of power between these two ancient adversaries has long since shifted in favour of humans.

Today the lust for crocodilian hides dominates the imbalance, and to meet the demand two million skins are harvested every year. The majority of these hides come from illegally poached crocodilians. Fortunately, crocodiles and alligators, unlike the elephant and rhinoceros, can be successfully farmed on relatively small tracts of land, and these farms, ranches and newly created breeding centres not only provide a ready resource for harvesting but also provide animals for reintroduction into natural habitats. There have already been two notable successes: the Indopacific or saltwater crocodile (*Crocodylus porosus*) in northern Australia and the American alligator (*Alligator mississippiensis*) in the United States. Both are protected and their populations in the wild have increased to such a point that they have been removed from CITES I and placed in CITES II. The profits from ranching are sufficiently high to encourage local governments to manage a sustainable harvest while preserving the species. Other efforts along these lines are also showing considerable promise, particularly in India where the mugger crocodile

(*C. palustris*) and the gharyal (*Gavialis gangeticus*) have made modest beginnings on the long path to survival.

It is ironic that the very thing that brought crocodilians to the edge of extinction, the value of their hides and the profit made from their sales, may end up by being their salvation. Most crocodilian conservationists express this view. One would have thought that the best way to save the crocodilians would be to enact a worldwide ban on the sale of skins, but this, like all simplistic solutions to the complex problems of animal conservation fails to consider both greed and ignorance. Thus, for the time being, the best strategy is to allow the skin trade to continue under careful, ever-increasing supervision. There is some promise in this direction, and people everywhere are becoming conscious of the need for preservation. Perhaps one day, in a more perfect world, people will no longer want belts, suitcases, pocketbooks and clothing made from crocodilian hides.

While hunting is still the primary threat to crocodilians, a second and more serious long-term threat to survival is human population growth. One famous biologist, in trying to explain the human population explosion, said 'After all, sex is the most fun you can have without laughing.' Given the cultural and religious taboos and ignorance about birth control, the basic problem is that there are too many people. The population problem is particularly acute in the developing nations where annual human population growths approach 5%. The result of this growth is that humans encroach on remaining natural habitats, building dams, irrigation canals, usurping nesting areas, draining swamps and reclaiming moist, marshy lowlands for agriculture. Another people/ crocodilian problem is that of competition. When human possessions, pets and cattle, or human life is endangered, the first human response is to kill. After all, we are the dominant species and, as such, hold our needs above those of all other organisms.

Fortunately, governments today have a more enlightened view of natural resources. Not only are crocodilians a renewable resource but also, like other giants of the Earth, they represent a significant tourist attraction and therefore are a valued commodity. Thus, in some respects, crocodiles can pay their own way. Pressure from international conservation groups is bringing about more allocations of protected lands in which crocodiles can thrive, and now, before development projects are begun, there is an increasing tendency for companies to make a statement about how the proposed development will affect animal and plant populations. The plight of crocodilians has finally been recognized.

One other factor that has a negative impact on crocodilians and many other endangered species (as well as on humans themselves) is pollution. Increased burning of rainforests and fossil fuels cause the production of acid rain which, in some areas, has already had sterilizing effects on lakes, ponds and marshes. The run-off of pollutants from heavily fertilized agricultural lands and the increasing use of toxic weed control chemicals and insecticides exacerbate the problem. We humans are finally beginning to recognize these threats and are responding to them, albeit slowly.

Whether we can save all 22 species of crocodilians is questionable. We are maintaining breeding stocks in farms and zoos, and there are a number of positive or promising programmes. Some wild populations will survive because their skins are so heavily armoured that they are useless as leather. Some will survive because they dwell in remote areas temporarily safe from human exploitation. And some will survive in national parks and on game reserves. But the vast numbers that only comparatively recently were found in tropical lands are a thing of the past. There is reason for hope, however, and if we manage wisely and carefully our greatgrandchildren's children will be able to experience the awe and delight of seeing these magnificent beasts in their preserved natural habitats.

*BELOW:* As living relics of prehistory, crocodiles arouse fear and fascination. They have become a significant tourist attraction; with good management, future generations will also be able to marvel at these mighty beasts.

# INDEX

Note: References to illustrations are
*italicized*. However there may be
textual references on the same
pages.

# SELECTED REFERENCES

D. Ackerman, 'A Reporter at Large: Crocodilians.' *New Yorker* 10 October 1988, 42–81.

J. L. Behler, *Crocodilians: Captive Culture and Crocodilian Advisory Group Recommendations.* (AAZPA Annual Proceedings 1989.)

J. L. Behler, P. Brazailis, K. B. Gercty and B. Foster, *Propogation of Crocodilians at the Bronx Zoo.* (11th International Herpetological Symposium on Captive Propagation and Husbandry, 1987.)

A. Bellairs, *The Life of Reptiles* (2 vols), Universe Books, New York 1970.

A. Bellairs and J. Altridge, *Reptiles,* Hutchinson, London 1975.

P. Brazailis, 'Identification of Living Crocodilians' *Zoologica* 58: 59–101, 1973.

A. Carr, 'Alligators: Dragons in Distress'. *National Geographic* 131: 133–148, 1967.

H. B. Cotl and A. C. Pooley, *Crocodiles: The Status of Crocodiles in West Africa.* (IUCN Publications paper 33, 1972.)

R. A. Coulson, J. Herbert and T. D. Coulson, 'Biochemistry and Physiology of Alligator Metabolism in Vivo', *American Zoologist* 29: 921–934, 1989.

F. M. Delaney and C. L. Abercrombie, 'American Alligator Food Habits', *Journal of Wildlife Management* 50: 348–353, 1986.

R. L. Dittmans, *The Reptiles of North America,* Doubleday, New York 1953.

C. Gans, 'Crocodilians in Perspective', *American Zoologist* 29: 1051–1054, 1989.

R. Gore, 'A Bad Time to be a Crocodile', *National Geographic* 153: 91–116, 1978.

A. Graham and P. Beard, *Eyelids of Morning: The Mingled Destinies of Crocodiles and Men,* A & W Visual Library, New York 1973.

E. Hoffman, 'Man Eaters!', *International Wildlife* Sept/Oct 1988.

J. A. Kushlan, 'Conservation and Management of the American Crocodile', *Environmental Management* 12: 777–790, 1988.

J. W. Lang and L. D. Garrick, 'Alligator Courtship', *American Zoologist* 15: 813, 1975.

J. W. Lang and L. D. Garrick, 'The American Alligator Revealed', *Natural History* 86: 54–61, 1977.

A. C. Pooley and C. Gans, 'The Nile Crocodile', *Scientific American* 234: 114–124, 1976.

K. R. Porter, *Herpetology,* W. B. Saunders, Philadelphia 1972.

C. A. Ross (ed.) *Crocodiles and Alligators,* Facts on File, New York 1989.

K. A. Vliet, 'Social Displays of the American Alligator', *American Zoologist* 29: 1019–1031, 1989.

# CREDITS

The author is indebted to the many crocodilian conservationists and researchers who kindly and enthusiastically contributed both their thoughts and their photographs, particularly John Behler of the Bronx Zoo, Romulus Whitaker of the Madras Crocodile Bank, Professor Kent Vliet of the University of Florida and Professor Jeffrey Lang of the University of North Dakota. Special thanks go to John Kearney for his novel ideas, editing and typing and to Miss Alison Levy of Donald Young Safaris for her photographs and help with research.

Photographs were supplied by the following sources: (l = left; r = right; c = centre; t = top; b = bottom.)

**Debbie Arrit** (US Fish and Wildlife Service): page 32.
**C. M. Dixon:** pages 35, 96. **Earthwatch:** pages 15 b, 70 b, 71 t.
**Elizabeth Godrock** (Boston University): pages 11 b, 122.
**Luther Goldman** (US Fish and Wildlife Service): page 11 t.
**Peter Jackson:** pages 21 t, 44 t, 47, 60 t, 60 b, 105, 106, 111, 114, 115, 117 t, 118 r, 125. **Jeffrey W. Lang** (University of North Dakota): pages 12, 26 b, 29, 30 t, 40 b, 64, 66, 67, 68 t, 69 t, 69 c, 70 t, 77, 78 t, 79 t, 84 t, 85 b, 94, 118 l. **Alison V. Levy:** pages 17, 27, 85 t, 85 c, 86 t, 86 c, 87 br, 88, 89 t, 89 b, 91, 97, 99 t, 102 t, 102 b, 121 t. **Charles Levy:** pages 3, 25, 36, 37 t, 37 b, 40 tl, 51 b, 53 t, 58, 68 b, 79 c. **Charles Levy/Frederica Matere:** page 14 b. **Joe McDonald:** page 123. **Metropolitan Museum of Art, NY:** page 39 t. **Origins Gallery, Brookline MA:** pages 33, 38 t, 38 b, 40 tr. **A. W. Palmisere** (US Fish and Wildlife Service): page 72 t. **Doug Perrine:** pages 13 t, 52, 57, 74 c, 120. **Photo/Nats:** cover images; pages 6, 7, 8, 13 b, 14 t, 28 t, 41, 46, 51 t, 59 t, 81, 100, 101, 124. **M. Pomeroy** (Boston University): pages 16, 24, 62 b. **Queensland National Parks and Wildlife Service:** pages 93, 108. **Ron Singer** (US Fish and Wildlife Service): page 80. **J. L. Tamarack:** pages 31 t, 53 b, 87 t. **R. Tamarin** (Boston University): page 19. **US Fish and Wildlife Service:** pages 26 t, 78 b, 83, 86 b, 87 bl. **US National Gallery:** page 39 b. **K. A. Vliet:** pages 15 t, 21 b, 28 b, 45 b, 50, 55 b, 61 t, 61 b, 62 t, 65, 69 b, 76 b, 84 b, 109. **Romulus Whitaker:** pages 18, 30 b, 48, 49 t, 49 b, 54, 55 t, 56, 59 b, 71 b, 72 b, 73, 74 t, 74 b, 75, 76 t, 90, 95, 98, 99 b, 103, 104 t, 104 b, 107, 116 t, 116 b, 117 b, 121 b.